MW01106194

*Sharon shows pr*

*to speak clearly to each ... ... ... ... ... ... ... ... ... ...*
*answer us, and she shows us how an "ordinary person just like me"*
*can hear from God for all our needs. Her transparency is refreshing.*
*"God Speaks...Are You Listening" will convince you that God does*
*speak and WILL answer you.*

Pat Bradley, CEO of Crisis Aid International

*What many call "coincidences," Sharon sees as God working and*
*acting in her life. She illustrates how God works and is very personal*
*in her daily life and challenges others to see how God wants to lead*
*their lives. No big theories, no complicated theological jargon, just*
*honest, straightforward testimony of how God can make a huge dif-*
*ference in our lives if we listen and act accordingly.*

Dr. David P. Hyatt, Christian Pastor, Coach and Consultant

*Jesus once said, "The sheep hear his voice, and he calls his own*
*sheep by name and leads them out...and the sheep follow him, for*
*they know his voice," (John 10:3-4 ESV). Tweets, texts, emails, Face-*
*book...the list continues to grow, overwhelming us with yet one more*
*way to simply communicate a message. Have you ever wondered if*
*and how God is speaking to us today? In "God Speaks...Are You Lis-*
*tening?" Sharon Marie Anderson engages each reader to enter into*
*her discovery of listening breakthroughs, while challenging us to dis-*
*cern and discover for ourselves the gentle voice of the Good Shepherd*
*who passionately desires to speak to His sheep, sharing a word of as-*
*surance, hope, direction, and grace.*

Pastor John Brunette, Faith Lutheran Church, St. Louis, MO

*There are no coincidences when it comes to God—sometimes He whispers, sometimes He shouts. In "God Speaks...Are You Listening?" you will stand in awe at the amazing ways that God speaks to Sharon and desires to speak to you. It will capture your mind to listen for the Lord's voice. It will give you a fresh, new glimpse at the many ways that the Lord desires to speak to you in your daily life. You will find yourself praying, "Lord, open the ears of my heart, so I can hear you speak more clearly."*

Joan Gangwer, MS, RD, LDN, CDE, Owner/Nutritionist

*John 10:27, "My sheep listen to my voice; I know them and they follow me." Sharon Marie Anderson writes from a heart of love for her God and with a desire to see the people of God walk in the fullness of John 10:27. Our shepherd is speaking to us daily and in "God Speaks...Are You Listening?", Sharon gives practical and helpful tips for how each of us can learn to hear the voice of God.*

Ruth Cox, CEO of Sheltering Wings, Burkina Faso, Africa

*Sharon Marie Anderson writes of a loving, personal God who not only cares for us, but understands us individually in a unique way. She takes us on her own spiritual journey, sharing personal stories of fear, doubt and triumph as she witnesses firsthand the presence of a sovereign God.*

*"God Speaks...Are you Listening?" is not simply one person's encounter with Jesus, but it implores the average follower of Christ to not only look and listen for God's presence, but to expect it!*

Dr. Jeffrey W. Anderson

*In "God Speaks...Are You Listening?", Sharon brings to light the constant pursuit God has for all of us. She shows us that when we take notice of the small things, or even the whispers God speaks in our everyday lives, we start to understand God's intentional plans for each of us. If anyone has ever pondered about what God has planned for their life, I encourage you to read this book and learn how God is speaking to you every day.*

Mike Riddering, Director of Sheltering Wings Orphanage, Yako, Burkina Faso, Africa

# GOD SPEAKS

## SPEAKS

*. . . are you listening?*

**Sharon Marie Anderson**

**God Speaks**...Are You Listening?
Sharon Marie Anderson

Published by Passionate Faith Ministry, LLC
St Louis, Missouri

Copyeditor: Lisbeth Tanz, www.lisbethtanz.com
Cover and Interior design: Cathy Davis, www.DavisCreative.com
Author photo: Warren Hertfelder, stlnikon@gmail.com

Library of Congress Cataloging-in-Publication Data
Library of Congress Control Number: 2015900219
Author: Sharon Marie Anderson
God Speaks...Are You Listening?
ISBN:978-0-9907419-0-9
Library of Congress subject headings:
    1. religion   2. christian life   3. general

Publication year 2015

# Dedication

Firstly, I dedicate this book and my life to God Almighty.
Our Heavenly Father has shown me his faithfulness, his grace,
his mercy, his forgiveness and his unconditional love.
My experiences have brought me closer to God, and I will never
be the same again. He is my Savior and my Redeemer.

Secondly, I dedicate this book to my loving husband and
soul mate. You are the most supportive, encouraging man
and a constant reminder to me of God's love.

I also dedicate this book to my children, grandchildren,
and family. You bring such joy and warmth to my life.
Your love is a constant reminder of God's blessings.

I hope that the stories you read help you in your
walk with the Lord and encourage you to remember
God's faithfulness and love in your own lives.

# Table of Contents

# ACKNOWLEDGEMENTS

So much goes into writing a book. I truly had no idea since this is my first one. I could never have pulled this off without the help of many, and I want to thank them all. I must first thank God. He is the one who has given me the stories to write from the experiences in my walk with Him. He has blessed me beyond words. He has truly given me daily inspiration and encouragement to step out of my "comfort zone" and follow him to help others come to know him more intimately.

To my loving husband John, I thank you for being patient as I worked many long hours in the office to finish this project. Your tireless encouragement to me, along with your desire to take care of all the other things in our life was such a relief and greatly appreciated. Your help on the business side of the book allowed me to keep focused on writing so that this project could continue to move forward.

I am extremely grateful to my friends and loved ones who encouraged me to write a book after taking the time to listen to my "God stories." To those friends who lifted me up in prayer for guidance, wisdom, and completion of the book, I thank you.

And, of course, there are those who helped me actually put the book together. I want to thank Cathy Davis, with **Davis Creative**, for first talking with me about my idea and my dreams for this book. You inspired me, walked me through the process, and coached me, while your beautiful work in graphic design made my book come alive. Thank you, Cathy, for your perspective and understanding of the image I wanted to create and for your patience.

I want to thank Lisbeth Tanz, at **The Hired Pen,** for her wonderful work of editing my book. I know you had a lot of "reworking" to do with my first book, and I appreciate all the hard work you put into making the book what it needed to be. Thank you for being patient with me when I called you numerous times for advice.

I would also like to thank Marcel Brown and Danelle Brown at **Queen Bee Consulting** for helping me with the marketing. Between the website and social media, you both were a tremendous help and a great resource to get me where I needed to be. You guided me through the crazy technology world, and I thank you.

Again, I could not have finished this book without the wonderful people who walked alongside me during the process. May God use this book to encourage others to faith, hope, and to hear Him speaking to them.

GOD BLESS!

*For God speaks again and again,*
*though people do not recognize it.*

JOB 33:14

# Introduction

*H*ave you ever had a thought and wondered where it came *from? Have you ever had someone speak something to you about a topic you were just pondering? Have you ever opened a book or magazine and read the answer to something you had been looking for? Have you ever turned on the television and felt almost immediately that the person on the screen is talking directly to you about a situation in your life?*

When these kinds of things happen to us, we tend to write them off as coincidences. We see them, we hear them, but we often ignore them. We tell ourselves that it is just too far-fetched to believe that something happened for a reason or that a person somehow knew what we needed to hear, just by "coincidence." This is a hard concept for most of us to grasp, that maybe, there is a God in heaven who knows us and is in control of everything here on earth.

If we believe this, however, does that mean we have no control over our lives? That doesn't set right with most of us! So, instead of making that "leap of faith," we dismiss the thought and tell ourselves that these "happenings" are just coincidences. Then we get on with controlling our lives, doing what we want when we want, and making all of our own decisions. We do this until something else happens that triggers the nagging feeling there is someone out there who knows our every thought and our every move. Again, we wonder if it could really be God in heaven speaking something into our lives, showing us what we need to do. Surely He has bigger problems and concerns in this world than to worry about little ole me and my little issues in life! How does he even know my name or where I live or what I am thinking about or what I am struggling with? We cower at the thought of being loved so much and cared for so much from someone we can't even see—a Father up in heaven who showers us with his grace, mercy, and unconditional love. The thought is too big for us, and it overwhelms us. It's just easier to dismiss it and go on with our lives as before.

Have you experienced times in your life where the "coincidences" seemed surreal and the circumstances almost too perfect to be explainable? Think back to one of those times. Can you imagine that it was orchestrated by God? Let that thought soak in. Could it really be true? Could God have been speaking to you through someone or some circumstance, and you just didn't make the connection at the time? Are you wondering why God would take the time to care about your life? Why He would want you to know the best path in life? Why He would care about your finances, your sick child, your career, or your broken-down car? Does thinking this way feel "too big?" Are you falling back into doubt that it's God reaching out? I ask that you suspend your disbelief at least for the time it takes you to read this book.

We truly have a Heavenly Father who wants to talk with us; He wants to let you know how much he loves you, and He will go to any lengths to get his thoughts and his ways across to you. He is all around us, but we aren't listening to Him. He speaks to us every day, but we are either too distracted with other things in our lives or our eyes are blind, and our ears can't hear. We pass off those "God moments" as coincidences, or think, "It's a small world," or do some other dismissive tactic instead of considering it could be our Heavenly Father guiding and directing us.

Here is a great example of God speaking through someone to me. Eight years ago, I met a pastor at a lunch with some friends. I had never met him before. As we sat there eating lunch, he turned to me and said, "Someday you are going to write a book and it is going to do very well." At the time, writing a book, much less writing anything, had never even crossed my mind. I said thank you and filed it away in the recesses of my mind. Looking back now, I realize those were words spoken from God through this pastor. Why else would someone whom I had never met before tell me I would write a book someday? My only explanation for this is God spoke words to him that he was to pass on to me, letting me know what God had planned for some time in my future. I pondered that statement for years but had no idea what I was supposed to do with it. Then one day, God spoke to me and told me to share my testimonies and stories about my life. I then had a clear vision and knew the appointed time was right to begin my writing career.

I hope the stories you read in this book spark a memory or two, give you pause for thought, and awaken your eyes and ears to "hear" when God is making His presence known to you. I am always amazed at the lengths God will go to when He wants us to be obedient to Him for His purposes. And his timing? It's always perfect.

*For God did not give us a spirit of fear,*
*but a spirit of power, love, and of self-discipline.*
2 TIMOTHY 1:7

CHAPTER ONE

# Africa

As so often happens, you ask one thing of God and He delivers something else that's much better. This is the beginning of my journey to Africa. It began on a Friday in October when I reached out to God in prayer asking for a clear sign as to whether my husband John was to go on his second mission trip to Uganda, Africa.

But first, a little back story. John and I had recently moved into our newly renovated home where I had spent a lot of my time co-ordinating projects, purchasing materials, and being the interior decorator, which is one of my passions in life. My husband and I are empty nesters, with four grown children from different marriages and one granddaughter. He established his own business years ago. I was no longer working, but volunteering my time with different organizations and helping needy families.

We had been on several mission trips to Mexico, but for the past three years, our mission field seemed to be in our hometown of St. Louis, Missouri. This made me happy because I was more of a stay-close-to-home and routine kind of person. I do not like to stray too far from my comfort zone. My husband is a world traveler, the farther away the better, the more unknown the better, the stranger the food the better. We're two very different people and personalities who just happen to be married.

It was the last week of September, and my husband had just returned from a mission trip to South Dakota. I stayed home, because this was a men-only mission. I had enjoyed my week visiting with friends and spending some time alone. While he was gone, I had time to think about his next mission trip in February. This one was much farther away—Uganda, Africa. Not surprisingly, I had some reservations about John leaving again. When he returned home from South Dakota, I expressed my feelings to him about his next trip. I told him there was plenty of "mission work" to do right here near our home, and that he didn't always have to run off somewhere else to do God's work. With a lot of urging from me, we decided to pray about whether or not John was to go on this mission trip or stay close to home with me. John needed to commit to the trip by October 11, so, with it already being late September, we hoped for a quick answer from God.

Now, being the prideful, stubborn, loving, get-my-way, supportive, controlling and ever so intuitive wife, I believed the answer would be in my favor. I figured that God would hear my prayer and let my husband stay home with me. That would be the best thing, at least for me. If he was home, I wouldn't have to worry about him

or be lonely for two weeks. In addition, he certainly had a lot of work to do right here, and I wouldn't feel guilty for not going, too. Besides, I justified, there are other people who can go to Africa to help. They won't miss one person.

I began to pray in earnest about Africa. "God, please give John and me a CLEAR SIGN as to whether he is supposed to go to Africa. We really need a CLEAR SIGN from you, so lay it right in front of us. Thank you in advance, Lord, for what you will show us."

There is an old saying, "Be careful what you ask for." John and I both learned that God delivers when you ask. Boy did He ever! In the weeks following our decision to pray about Africa, we did get a CLEAR SIGN (actually SIGNS), mainly directed at ME!

A week had passed, yet there was no clear sign from God about Africa. Since it was Sunday, we headed to church. The pastor leading the sermon was Pastor Drew, a young man, but a very vibrant speaker and truly anointed by God. He was a newcomer to our church, hired to lead church missions. On this day, his sermon was on Ephesians 3:14-21. However, he focused a great deal on verse 20 during his sermon.

> *Now to him (God) who is able to do*
> *immeasurably more than all we ask or imagine,*
> *according to his power that is at work within us.*

We listened and took notes, and went about our day after the service ended.

That evening, as my husband and I were reading, he interrupted my train of thought to tell me he had just read the same scripture (Ephesians 3:20) in his devotional. I mumbled, "OK" and went back to my reading. The next morning, the same verse was in another daily devotional we read. After reading it, John exclaimed, "You are not going to believe this, but here is that same scripture again, and it's talking about Uganda, Africa in the story." For John, seeing the same scripture three times in 24 hours was a definite sign. The mention of Uganda, Africa in the daily devotional story was the metaphysical "icing on the cake." He felt strongly that there were no coincidences happening but signs from God that he was supposed to go on the Africa trip. I half heartedly agreed. I was not completely convinced that was what those signs meant, but I was deluding myself. I refused to believe that I wasn't going to get my way, meaning John would stay home with me. Little did I realize that God was not only nudging John in the right direction. I had no idea that I was really the focus of God's intent—and getting my attention was no easy task!

That afternoon, I was with a friend working on the fourth week of our Bible study called *Experiencing God*. As we studied, pains began in the right side of my stomach. It was mild at first, but increased in intensity over the next two hours. As the pain worsened, I prayed for it to go away. By late afternoon, the pain diminished and was gone. I couldn't explain it, especially since I woke up feeling great the next day. I felt so good I decided to go take a spinning class. After cleaning up, I was picked up by a friend. We had plans to paint the walls at an antique gallery where John and I rented a space. About an hour into painting, the pain on my right side came back with a vengeance. It hurt badly, and I tried to ignore it. I continued painting, thinking it would pass after a couple of hours as before. Not only did the pain not subside, I started feeling warm. Despite a cool room temperature, sweat droplets began running down my back. I had to get off my ladder—and quick! The pain in my side was growing more intense, so I went to the car to rest. Worried, my friend walked with me. As I sat down, my whole body broke into an intense sweat. My friend watched as sweat traced paths down my face. If it had been hot outside, sweating would have made sense. But it was October, and the air was crisp. My clothes were soaked by the time my sweating attack ended. Happily, the pain in my side was gone, too. We decided painting could wait until another day, and my friend drove me home. I called John to tell him what had happened. He insisted I make an appointment with my doctor ASAP. Luckily, I was able to see the doctor that evening.

After I described my attack to him, he said, "You really aren't a candidate for gallstones, but it sounds like that's what it could be." He recommended blood work and an ultrasound the next day, which I did. I was taking it easy around the house after my ultrasound, when I felt a strange urge to go into my office and read one of my health books. I had no idea which one to choose as I have three shelves full of health and nutrition books. God must have been directing me because, as I stood in front of my bookcase, my hand went directly to a book entitled, *The Acid, Alkaline Balance Diet.*

I had bought it over a year ago and had only read bits and pieces of it before, noting interesting parts with several bookmarkers.

Curious what I might find, I opened it and started reading at one of the places I had marked before. It was describing what intestinal disorders are like and what causes them. Intriguing! My reading was interrupted by John's return from work. I put the book down and chatted with him for a while. When I started reading again, I clearly heard a whisper, "Turn back two pages." This was odd, but I turned back two pages. The heading almost leapt off the page. There, in bold black print was the word, "GALLSTONES." I had paged through this book before but I didn't remember seeing a heading for Gallstones. Figuring I was lead to this page for a reason, I began reading. About halfway down the second page it stated, "...and the tribes living near Lake Victoria in UGANDA, AFRICA, collect the now-inorganic remains of large winged insects..." I was stunned. Did I really just read that? How is it that I pick a random book, get a message to turn back two pages, begin reading about gallstones, and end up with a story about Uganda, Africa?

Uganda, Africa. I'm certain I stared at those words with my mouth open. Coincidence? Synchronicity? No, it wasn't any of those things. In that moment I knew, beyond the shadow of a doubt, that God was speaking to me through this book and the recurring Bible verse. He did this to show me how much he wanted John to go to Africa, and that He was not going to let me mess this one up. He had plans for John to be in Uganda, and He had to show me by making me sick, as He often does when He is trying to teach me something. God knows that I value my health above almost anything. He knows he can get my attention in this way, and He always does.

Once I recovered from my shock, I went searching for John. I showed him the book and the passage about Uganda under Gallstones, and I told him he had my blessing to go on the trip. In fact, I wanted to put him on a plane right away so that God knew I got it. Well, that and I was hoping to stave off anything else happening to my health.

A week later, I received my test results and, not surprisingly, they were all negative for gallstones. My blood work was perfect; there was no detection of gallstones on the ultra-sound, and I had not had any stomach pain recurrence. Thank you, God. Message received. I had no reason to think God had anything else to relay to me about Africa. I was wrong.

*He who has ears, let him hear.*
Matthew 11:15

I can be rather impatient. Waiting has never been my strong suit. I found myself, on October 9, waiting for a technician to install a phone line. My appointment was between 1:00 p.m. and 3:00 p.m. Sure enough, he pulled in promptly at 3:00. As we discussed the work to be done, I couldn't help but notice his beautiful accent. When I asked where he was from, I was startled to hear, "Africa." He explained, "I was born in New York City, but at a very young age I moved with my parents to Africa. I just recently moved back to the States." I almost laughed aloud. After all the signs John and I had received about Africa, here was another one standing in my kitchen. It didn't matter that he wasn't Ugandan.

As we talked, I shared the news about John going on a mission trip to Africa. The tech told me how much he would like to go back there to help people. He talked about how much need there is and asked me to give my husband his phone number so he could tell him what he knows about it.

After he left, I called John at work. I began with, "You will never believe what just happened!" and proceeded to tell him the story. We laughed about it and wondered why God didn't seem to understand that we knew John was supposed to go to Africa. We were puzzled as to why this had happened. Since we knew there wasn't an answer to our question, we let it go.

A few days passed. On a quiet Sunday evening, I finished the homework for Day 5 of Unit 4 in my *Experiencing God* Bible study workbook. After finishing, I decided to read over Unit 5. The first thing I saw after turning the page was, "GOD SPEAKS" written in bold. Underneath was written, "God's Activity in Africa." Again, I found myself wondering why God persisted in showing me things about Africa. I was impressed with His determination to repeatedly show me things about Africa. So, with the same kind of determination, I read every word that this message had to say. It began with Zambia and the suffering of the millions of AIDS orphans there. It talked about churches in the United States that ministered to this enormous need. It went on to talk about how one missionary shared his story and the amazing results that were realized from that sharing. It finished by stating we have no idea what God can do through our lives and how our every conversation with God has limitless possibilities.

That wasn't all. The last line of the last paragraph on this page was the same scripture, Ephesians 3:20, that John had read three times in 24 hours that convinced him he was supposed to go to Africa. A gentle breeze would have blown me over like a feather.

*Now to him (God) who is able to do immeasurably more than all we ask or imagine, according to his power that is at work within us.*

I now have this scripture memorized for life, and I am not very good at memorizing scriptures! I knew that God had something big planned, and for some reason, He kept showing it to me. I shared this newest revelation with John, and then we retired for the night.

On Monday morning, I headed to my friend's house for Bible study. I couldn't wait to share my finding with her about Unit 5. She knew about all the "Africa" messages John and I had been receiving. My first words to her were, "Can you believe the story in Unit 5 about Africa? Were you surprised that it had the same Bible verse as what John saw?" My excitement grew to confusion as I waited for her response. She looked at me blankly and asked me what I was talking about. I said, "You know, the story on the first page of Unit 5 about Africa!" She responded, "My workbook doesn't say anything about Africa on Unit 5."

We both paused, and then hurried to open our workbooks. My friend had done this Bible study before and, to save money, was using her workbook from the prior year. I purchased a new workbook before we started to study together. Turns out, the Unit 5 stories are completely different. Mine talked about Africa; hers talked about a town in Canada. This unit was the only one that was different ... we checked. There was no logical explanation for this difference, yet it was there in black and white.

Others might pass this off as coincidence. Again, I say this was no coincidence. It was God speaking, and it sure made me sit up and take notice. But why again? I was still wondering where it was all going. What was God trying to tell us? We knew John was supposed to go to Africa, so why the persistence?

Sometimes friends say the craziest things. That day, my dear friend and study buddy, said, "Sharon, maybe you are supposed to go to Africa also!" I almost choked as the words came out of her mouth. I replied, "Not me, oh! That is just crazy. I don't want to go to Africa; I am afraid to go to Africa. That can't be what this is about!" After my outburst, I stopped and said aloud, "What if it is? Why would God call me to Africa?" I tried to support my position of not wanting to go by reasoning, "He knows I like to stay in my comfort zone. That is how he made me, right? He knows I have my mission work right here. He knows my husband likes to travel to faraway places, not me. There must be another explanation for this, and I am sure it has nothing to do with me." My friend embedded the thought that I must have to go to Africa, too, unwittingly, perhaps. Now that it's there, I have to ponder it. I don't like it, I am not sure at this point if I like her anymore, and I certainly don't like what she said. However, the realization is, something is going on!

For the next seven days, everywhere I turned I saw and read things that pertained to fear and worry. I have always struggled a lot with fear and worry. One of the things that I fear most is losing my health, despite a healthy diet and a strong exercise ethic. Because I have always enjoyed feeling good and being healthy, I was fearful of putting anything into my body that I thought might be unhealthy or dangerous. For a while, I thought I had control of my health. I learned the hard way how foolish this belief was and that, instead, God is the one in control of everything, including our health. He can give it to us at anytime, and He can take it away at anytime. All we can do is our best to take care of our temples in a way pleasing to God.

I knew I needed to address my fear and worry. I read, I prayed, I walked and talked with God about it. I knew I shouldn't worry about anything, I knew I shouldn't fear anything, so why did I? Why was I afraid to go to Africa? Was it the distance? Was it the food? Was it the unknown? Was it the sickness and diseases? Was it the language barrier? Was it the necessary immunizations? Yes, yes, and yes! I realized I feared all of those things. I knew God wouldn't want me to worry or fear any of those things. He wanted me to have faith in Him and go into the world to help the poor and needy.

All week long, I kept thinking about these issues and wondered if I was being selfish and self-centered for wanting to stay in my own little comfort zone. I didn't find any easy answers, and God wasn't finished with me on the subject yet, either.

A week later, and one day before John and I were to leave to visit family in Philadelphia, I had lunch with another friend. I don't talk with her often, so this lunch was a treat. I was anxious to share my Africa stories with her; I wanted to see her reaction. At her request, we met at a restaurant of her choosing.

After exchanging pleasantries and ordering our food, I said, "You're not going to believe what has been happening in my life lately!" I launched into my story. I wasn't even halfway through it when she said, "Sharon, you are not going to believe this!" I braced myself. I've learned when someone says this, it's usually going to be some huge, humdinger of a lesson for me!

While waiting for me in front of the restaurant, she had strolled to the storefront next door. It was a travel agency. As she walked closer, the window display caught her eye. It was about AFRICA! She admitted the display got her thinking about how awesome a trip to Africa would be to experience. She thought I might want to go, too. I was shocked; first, because she thought going to Africa would be awesome and second, because she thought I would agree!

I clearly didn't want to go to Africa, but at this point, I was beginning to be afraid not to go to Africa! I explained that John was going, and I really had no desire to go. With tears in her eyes, she said, "Why wouldn't you go and experience that with your husband? I am sure he would be so excited if you went with him. Why wouldn't you do that?" I opened my mouth to reply, but found no words. Then I quietly mumbled, "Fear!" There, I had said it; and it sounded so stupid. Why was I so fearful to go, while all she could see was how awesome it could be? Hadn't God been showing me over the past week to have faith and trust in Him? Hadn't I learned that fear and worry were sins? My appetite was gone, and I sat dejected. I knew I was fighting a losing battle with God. It was suddenly clear—He wanted me to go to Africa. He was certainly persistent about it. This was a lunch I wasn't going to forget anytime soon.

For the rest of the day, I was immersed in thought about this revelation. I decided the best course of action was to give in and submit to God's will, even though part of me was still questioning why.

John's reaction to my new understanding was, let's just say, anticlimactic. He was silent as I admitted I still didn't quite believe this was really what God wanted. I didn't sleep well that night. I felt exhausted as I crawled out of bed the next morning. I still had packing to do for the trip. I was feeling weighed down with this big decision. All I wanted to do was run away from it. I just wanted to concentrate on packing, forget everything else, and get on the road. That was not God's plan.

Instead, the first thing I felt led to do was go to my computer and print off *Prime Time with God*, a daily devotional email I receive. Once again, God surprised me. I almost couldn't believe my eyes.

## TODAY'S PRAYER

*God, I pray that you take me out of my comfort zone. I pray that you break my heart to pieces for the poor and needy so that I will be driven beyond belief to look after them like you would. Forgive me for being so self centered. Forgive me for being all about me, myself, and I. Forgive me for my stupid, ridiculous opinions while people that you love and cherish suffer due to my inaction and selfish attitude. God raise me up into a person of compassion and love like you are. Amen.*

This was exactly the kind of "in your face" style God needed to use with me. Having my selfish attitude so brazenly stated was too much for me. My throat closed and the tears fell in buckets. I sat at my computer and wept with gulping sobs. I couldn't believe that God had so clearly spoken to me. He showed how much He cared about me. More importantly, He emphasized His great love for the forgotten poor and needy and that He wanted and needed me to look after them like He would. If that doesn't bring someone to his or her knees, nothing will. It was at that moment, after I stopped crying, I finally knew I had to go to Africa. The Lord wanted me there for a reason. I didn't know why He had chosen me, but I knew I was going.

Writing this story brought back all the crazy feelings I had over those several weeks. I am still in awe of how God very patiently gave me sign after sign after sign until He had to hit me over the head to get his point across. I had gotten it … finally!

My husband and I finished packing and began the long drive to Philly. I figured at some point I needed to tell him the decision I had made. I knew he would be excited about it, but also skeptical. He was excited all right, but then asked if I was going to back out as it got closer. How dare him! I had just made the biggest decision in my life to step so far out of my comfort zone! I asked him why he would think that I'd back out. He looked at the road, glanced at me, then back to the road. He mumbled, "Guatemala." OK, that was a fair point. At the last minute, I had backed out of Guatemala, the first mission trip we were supposed to go on together. The issue at that time was immunizations. I couldn't handle putting toxic stuff into my body. It's my temple; I care for it and don't put bad or unhealthy things into it. I certainly wasn't going to break that rule for a silly mission trip. I quickly assured him that I would not back out. Truthfully, I was more afraid to stay home and not go than I was to go on the trip. Being obedient to God was more important to me than getting my own way.

As we drove along, my mind was flooded with questions. What if, after I just made this big decision, there wasn't room for me on this mission trip? The team had already had their meeting about the trip, and I knew that there were a limited number of spaces available because of flight reservations and accommodations. In fact, I was sure that it was full already. How would I fit in? This was a medical mission trip, so would they need someone else along who wasn't a medical person? Finally, could this maybe be my way out? What if there was just no room for me, or they needed another nurse or doctor on the trip? I had said, "Yes" to the trip; I was still being obedient to God. Maybe that's all He wanted. My heart beat a little faster. If that was true, then God was going to let me out of this one! Yes! I had an out! I almost fist pumped the air. John brought me back to reality with, "Of course there will be room for you if God wants you to go!" Despite my continued concerns, I knew deep in my heart God wanted me to go!

> *For I know the plans I have for you, declares the*
> *Lord, plans to prosper you and not to harm you,*
> *plans to give you hope and a future. Then you will*
> *call upon me and come and pray to me, and I will*
> *listen to you. You will seek me and find me when*
> *you seek me with all your heart.*
> Jeremiah 29:11-13

I am constantly in awe still about how personal God is with us. He can speak to us through so many different forms of communication, television, books, magazines, people, radio, and that small whisper we hear when we are listening. But are we listening? First, you have to believe that God wants to speak to you before you will tune your ears in to His voice. He wants that relationship with you desperately. You need to know that.

Then, you have to believe that God will speak to you and start to recognize the ways in which He will do that with you. Start by being aware of things said to you, of thoughts that just pop into your head, or something you may be reading in a book or magazine, and then say a little prayer asking God to help you discern it. Then, once you have been given a word from the Lord, you must try to be obedient to whatever He has imparted to you.

## POINTS TO PONDER

Signs, Signs, Signs, they are everywhere. God speaks to us in a variety of ways. He will use things in our lives that He knows will get our attention to help us step out of our comfort zones and focus on what He has planned for us. Has God spoken to you in any of these ways?

- Through physical pain or an unexpected health issue? What lesson did you learn from it?

- Convicting you of a "fear" issue you need to deal with? What other fears have you not turned over to the Lord?

- Taking you into "unknown" territory where you need to be completely reliant on God? How did you feel when you had to step out in faith?

- Breaking your heart for something close to His heart? Did it encourage you to reach out and help in some way?

Stop and ponder for a moment an event in your life where you felt God was speaking to you.

*The Lord himself goes before you and will be*
*with you; he will never leave you nor forsake you.*
*Do not be afraid; do not be discouraged.*

Deuteronomy 31:8

CHAPTER TWO

# Being a Pincushion

Our visit to Philadelphia was wonderful. We had a great time visiting with family. We had lunch with Jeff, John's brother, and Doug after church on Sunday. I shared my "God" story with our table. Everyone listened intently, and John's brother even shed a few tears, as he knew how big a step going to Africa was for me. After I had finished my story, I asked if there was still an opening available for me. The interesting answer again shows God's power and glory.

Doug, the CEO of Covenant Mercies, said, "About three days ago,"—(which would have been Thursday, the day I read *Prime Time with God* and wept) "a nurse dropped out of the trip. This was not a problem as we already had enough medical people on the trip. What we need is a "non-medical" person to go instead to help organize and administrate." He then looked directly at me and said, "Yes, a spot is open for you, perfectly orchestrated by God." That was it; I was in! I was going to Africa.

After a leisurely visit in Philadelphia, we headed home. At some point during our drive, John subtly reminded me that I needed to start the immunization process as soon as possible. I asked him to fill me in on just what I needed to get for this trip. He named off five or six different shots. With this news, my heart rate increased and sweat started dripping down my back. I worked hard not to panic. I knew I had to do it, so I made my first appointment with a travel doctor after we arrived home.

On the day of my appointment, I was fine until the doctor walked in. I always get the "white coat syndrome" whenever I am in a doctor's office. He was nice enough, for a guy who was going to give me my first immunization. He asked me a few questions about where I was going to travel and why. OK, I remember thinking, enough small talk let's get on with it. Today was the big one, at least in my mind, yellow fever vaccine! I had to get this to get a visa to enter the country. The nurse came in, my heart started to race, my blood pressure began to rise … and then it was over. Well, that wasn't so bad! She told me I could have some flu-like symptoms over the next 24 to 48 hours, but that not everyone gets them. As I walked to my car, I prayed that God wouldn't let me get sick. He didn't, that time.

I waited two weeks to get my first-ever flu vaccination. I didn't want the irony of coming down with the flu after getting all the other vaccines. I was determined that the flu was not going to stop me from going to Africa. Despite my best intentions, that is almost what happened. I let two more weeks pass, then I was immunized against typhoid and tetanus.

## Sick? Me?

With only one shot to go, I was feeling good both mentally and physically. I had weathered all of them better than expected. I hadn't had any flu-like symptoms or sore arms, nor any apparent scars or wounds, either. Just as I began to think the whole immunization thing was a piece of cake, my back went out ten days after my last shot. My back hadn't had any major problems in seven years. I was in terrible pain and, to add insult to injury, it happened with only five days until Christmas. So much to do, not enough time left to do everything and my back goes out. Now what was this all about? I know God has control over everything, but I couldn't see what the problem was.

Didn't He see my devotion and dedication over the last month and a half with getting all those shots? Why was He letting this happen to me now, when He took such great care of me before? I understand that He does everything out of love for us and that it's always for the best. However, I couldn't see that then, but I knew it was happening for a reason.

My back was in and out for five or six days. Then, like magic, it was fine again. Christmas was over and we were fast approaching the New Year. It was cold and dreary outside, and the flu bug was running rampant in St. Louis. Since I'd had the flu shot, I offered to watch my granddaughter who had come down with a particularly nasty strain of influenza. I learned the hard way that flu shots are only effective if they target the right strain.

Sure enough, two days later, I started to feel funny. I knew I was getting sick! The flu hit hard and fast. Just two hours later, I was running to the bathroom, sweating profusely, and feeling as if I wanted to die. The fever and sweats continued into the night until the wee hours of the next morning. I had never been this sick before. I couldn't believe after all the shots I'd had, including the flu shot that I felt this incredibly awful. We were just three weeks out from our trip to Africa. I was physically and emotionally spent. Again, I went to God in prayer.

My flu bug lasted a total of five days. I continued to ask God what He was trying to show me. I pleaded with Him to help me feel better, but I was getting discouraged. With just a little over two weeks until our big departure, I wanted to feel good and be excited about my mission trip.

## Baptism

John and I decided to get a total submersion baptism before we went to Africa. Our church didn't have this capability, but we located a church not too far away that was putting the finishing touches on their baptismal pool. It was to be finished by the Sunday prior to our departure. We decided to go ahead with our plan, acknowledging it was really God's plan for us. My throat began to feel scratchy the day before our baptism. Nothing serious, I was sure it would go away. As the day wore on, I started feeling funny again as if some illness was trying to take hold inside me. I brushed it off, declaring that nothing was going to stop me from being baptized tomorrow. I woke up Sunday morning still feeling a little funny. I looked outside. It was 20 degrees with snow flurries. This was not the best day to be completely submerged in water even though it is inside of the church, I thought.

We learned when we arrived at the church that the baptismal pool was inside of the church—it just wasn't in a heated part. Even more concerning, the water was a "balmy" 50 degrees. This was not welcome news.

I already felt as if I was coming down with something, and now I was going to be dunked in a cold pool, then stand in an even colder room. "Lord, give me strength," I whispered. Backing out wasn't an option; we had invited numerous friends and family to witness it. In we went. Boy was it cold.

That evening, sitting in my living room, I was still shivering from earlier in the day. I had several blankets on me, and my three cats were happily snuggled in. I noticed my nose was stuffy, my throat a little scratchy. I so didn't want a cold!

I awoke Monday morning with a full-blown, head-pounding, nose-stopping cold! Not again! Why me, and why now? I had to leave in five days for Africa. I had never had so many illnesses in such a short period. In fact, I'm hardly ever sick.

So many questions! I started a conversation with God, hoping for answers. All I heard back from Him was "Trust me. I have it under control; you are in my hands." I knew God had it under control, and I knew that I was going to get on that plane no matter what! I was a little angry and depressed for a couple of days, even though I knew this is where God wanted my faith to grow. He wanted me to lay my life completely and totally in His hands; to know that He knew what was best for me and that He would watch over me. This was a hard lesson for me, but one that had to be learned.

> *But those who hope in the Lord will renew their*
> *strength. They will soar on wings like eagles;*
> *they will run and not grow weary,*
> *they will walk and not be faint.*
> Isaiah 40:31

I tried to be in a good mood as I packed for the trip, all the time hoping and praying that I would wake up the morning of the flight feeling wonderful! Well, God had more faith building in me to do. On the morning we left, I still had the cold but knew I was nearing the end of it. My husband and I flew overnight to London and checked into our hotel the next morning.

After taking a short nap, we ventured out to see the London sights. We ate a hearty lunch and decided to keep walking to get a little exercise. The air was chilly, and a snowflake fell here and there. We wondered how unusual snow was for London. A friendly local assured us that all they ever see is a few flakes and never any accumulation. We enjoyed our leisurely stroll around London, but we talked excitedly about the next leg of our trip. Snow was still falling when we went to bed, but we didn't think much of it.

The next morning we were greeted with six to eight inches of snow—the biggest snow London had seen in 18 years! The city was ill equipped to deal with that much white stuff; consequently, the entire city simply shut down. Eight hundred flights in and out of London were cancelled that day. Businesses and schools closed, and people were stranded everywhere.

Our hotel was connected to the airport, which gave us a unique vantage point to view the mayhem. I have never seen so many people in one airport before. Everyone was trying to reschedule their flights. People were lined up for at least a half-mile trying to snag a hotel room and get a little rest. It was truly a mess!

How was it that John and I had two days to spend in London before flying on to Africa, and the whole city shuts down from the biggest snowstorm in 18 years? We never figured that one out. The rest of our team was due to arrive the next day, but it wasn't clear if the airport would be back to normal by then, or if the team would be on time. Then we remembered that nothing is impossible with God. We began to pray. Our team arrived on the second flight to land, on time. God is good! That same evening, the whole team boarded the plane headed to Entebbe, Africa. Our adventure was truly beginning!

## Africa ... Finally

The plane ride to Entebbe was uneventful, the best kind of flight. Safely in Entebbe, we boarded our bus for the nine- to ten-hour drive to Kamwenge, where we would be staying. It actually ended up being more like a 12- to 13-hour drive because of rain and muddy roads. Between nodding on and off, from lack of sleep, there were some interesting sites to be seen.

Kampala, a larger city, was so incredibly crowded. Between pedestrians, cars and bikes, there wasn't an inch of room. Rush hour in St. Louis has nothing on this city! Contrasting with the big cities were all the little villages and mud huts where people lived their lives in what we would call poverty. It was a humbling and an eye-opening experience for me. To see the lack of things that we take for granted everyday was astonishing. No electricity, no running or clean water, dirt roads, no cars, and a hole in the ground for a bathroom.

Yet, they came out of their homes smiling and waving at the "Muzungus" (white people) driving by in the bus. I was impressed with that; they have so little and yet appeared to be so friendly and happy! (A fun and silly experience involved standing on the equator. The water really does swirl clockwise in the northern hemisphere and counter-clockwise in the southern.)

We arrived at our guesthouse in Kamwenge around 11:00 p.m. on Wednesday night. We were exhausted. Our modest room was dimly lit with one light bulb in the ceiling. There was a double bed with mosquito netting over it, one table and a "bathroom." It had a semi-flushing toilet, a small sink, and a round, shallow bucket on the floor to take a "shower" in. There were two small windows up high, with no screens, hence, the mosquito netting over the bed. I took all this in while thinking, "This is our home for the next nine days." I was almost too tired to care about the sparse accommodations, but I remember laughing and saying that God was really stretching my faith on this trip! We went to bed, knowing that we had to get up by 6:00 a.m. to set up the medical clinic and start seeing people by 11:00 a.m.

## Sleep? What sleep?

John and I are used to sleeping in a king-size bed at home. John is not a little guy; he is 6'1" and 200 pounds of muscle. But there we were, crammed next to each other into a double bed, his feet hanging off the end. We had one sheet and blanket, small pillows, and no fan.In addition, we were sleeping under a mosquito net, which was tucked in as tightly as possible, because I was afraid of the mosquitoes in Africa. John fell asleep within two seconds, but I was wide-awake wondering how I was ever going to get to sleep. On top of that, I sleep on my side and usually toss and turn through the night. With my inability to move freely, I felt like a sardine stuffed into a can. This wasn't going to work, and I prayed for an answer!

Two nights later, after I had accumulated maybe ten hours of sleep in three nights, I asked the woman running the guesthouse if we could have another mattress or anything for my husband to sleep on. She delivered a couple of foam pieces to the room. I thank the Lord He gave me an awesome, loving, respectful, caring, sensitive, wonderful husband who would do anything in the world for me, because I pointed at the foam pieces on the floor and told him that was his new bed for the remainder of the trip. I think he was actually fine with this new arrangement because I was starting to get crabby from my lack of sleep.

We hung a new mosquito net from the ceiling and used one of our suitcases to elevate it on one end so it was away from his face. He slept pretty well down there, and I slept like a baby in that double bed by myself, tossing and turning side to side all night long. I definitely thanked God for good sleep, which re-energized me for the rest of the trip.

*Not only so, but we also rejoice in our sufferings,*
*because we know that suffering produces perseverance;*
*perseverance, character; and character, hope.*
Romans 5: 3-4

## Bats with Dinner

During this amazing trip, God continually showed me His grace, mercy, and faithfulness. All of our meals, which were delicious, were cooked and served by the native women there. This was a step out in faith for me, knowing that we could get sick from food we were not used to eating. But God watched over every one of us, and not one person got sick from the food or anything else!

God also provided bats. These winged mouse-like creatures literally hung upside down over our dinner table every night. Most people would be disgusted by this, but those tiny bats were a blessing because they love to eat mosquitoes. Our dinner area was open to the night air; nighttime is when the malaria-infested mosquitoes come out. Having the bats meant we ate in peace, and the bats were well fed. Other than watching out for bat drippings on the food, it was a pleasure to have them "hang out" with us.

## Medical Clinic

The first three days of the medical clinic were inspirational for me. There must have been more than 250 people each day waiting to be seen by a doctor or dentist. They would walk to the clinic, sit on wood benches under a makeshift canopy, and wait sometimes eight hours to see a doctor. Most of them had no food or water with them, and they never complained. They graciously and humbly sat there and smiled at us, just so thankful that we were there to help them. The people of Kiburara taught all of us a lot about genuine appreciation. They have so little and are such thankful people. The children were happy, smiling, and dancing around, at least the mostly healthy ones. Other children could barely hold their heads up, as they suffered from things such as dehydration, hunger, HIV, or malaria. Seeing these children in such dire conditions with life-threatening illnesses made me stop and consider how blessed we are in the United States to have medical care so easily accessible.

Sunday morning arrived, and we boarded the bus to travel to Kiburara, a 20-minute drive from Kamwenge, to attend a church service. During the bus ride, John and I didn't sit by one another. I decided to talk with two women in the group, so I sat across from them. The bus was constructed with one seat on the left of the aisle and two seats on the right. I sat down on the one-seat side so I could talk with my friends.

Ten minutes into the trip, while deep in conversation, a bunch of papers landed in my lap and then spilled onto the floor. Stunned because I had no idea where they had come from, I looked around quickly. I spied a binder on the rack above my friends' heads. I assumed the papers had fallen out of the binder. I reached down to gather them up so that I could put them back. I continued to talk as I straightened up the large number of pages. I happened to look down at the top sheet before I stood up to put them away. It read, "Gallstone Evaluation." I was speechless. I almost couldn't move for a second. I looked down again to make sure I had not imagined what I just saw. The paper that landed on top, by no authority of mine, read "Gallstone Evaluation."

I never imagined after my own potential gallstone diagnosis that I would see a paper entitled "Gallstone Evaluation." I believe God wanted me to know that He was right there with me, to be afraid of nothing, that He was in control and that He knew me personally and cared for me. **I believe He is there for every one of us in that same way and wants to communicate with us desperately every day.** We just need to be obedient and have a personal relationship with Him daily. He truly does speak to us, and I love to hear from Him.

## POINTS TO PONDER

Whatever we go through in life, God wants us to know that He is always there for us, especially as we experience "unpleasant" circumstances. His love and protection never leave us even during trials. We must continue to trust God and rely on His faithfulness.

- Do you trust God in all aspects of your life? In what area do you still need to trust Him?

- Are you able to remain "steady and unwavering" in trying circumstances? Why do you think that you sometimes "waver" during trials in your life?

- Do you look at trials in life as lessons to be learned? What trial in your life has caused a change in you?

- Are you willing to give up control of your life to God? What area of your life are you still holding on to?

Take a few minutes to "be still" and ask God to show you how to trust Him more through life's trials.

*I lift up my eyes to the hills—where does my*
*help come from? My help comes from the Lord,*
*the Maker of heaven and earth.*
Psalm 121: 1-2

## CHAPTER THREE

# The Bar, The Pain, and Jonah

G oing to Africa wasn't the first time I'd been directed by the wisdom of God. That started much earlier in my life.

I've spent a good deal of my life chasing the "things" of this world. I was never happy, and I punctuated my unhappiness by getting my first divorce in 1986, when my first child was five years old and my second only 18 months.

Despite my expectation that everything would be better, I continued to be unhappy and discontent with my life. This was despite having everything I thought I wanted: a new marriage to a wonderful man, a new house and a successfully blended family. Life was good! The goodness didn't last. I became discontented again. I didn't know the Lord yet, so the "things" in the world were what I focused on wanting. In addition, I had become restless in my marriage.

It was at this point one of my clients began talking with me about the Lord. I attended her church a couple of times and even went to a Bible study with her. She had given me a Bible, and I started reading it a little. I can honestly say I did feel that God was trying to speak to me. I would see little signs of this, but I was still too stubborn and hard-hearted to listen. I had made up my mind that getting divorced, again, was the best thing for me. Truth be told, back then it was always all about me! I truly didn't care who I was about to hurt. I wish I had listened to God in those days. But I didn't, so I faced the consequences of disobedience. I learned, though, that He is a Loving Father who can be trusted despite our sinful behavior.

My second divorce was not easy; no divorce ever is. My soon-to-be former husband was not on board with the idea. Consequently, I had to move out of the house we shared and live in a cramped, two-bedroom apartment with my 15-year-old daughter. She was unhappy that we had to leave her childhood home. I assured her it wouldn't be for too long, because I was hoping to get the house in the divorce. It wasn't that I loved the house so much. I was a fitness trainer, and I worked with most of my clients at my basement home gym. In order to continue supporting myself, I had asked for the family home as part of the divorce agreement. This was a sticking point in our divorce, which took longer than I expected to resolve.

I had forgotten what living "on your own" meant. I naively thought everything would be perfect. I neglected to consider that I had to support my daughter and myself for the first time in almost fourteen years. I quickly learned that it wasn't going to be easy as money was tight. Fortunately, after only living in the apartment a couple of weeks, I ran into some friends who owned a bowling alley that included a small bar on the other side. They told me they needed a bartender on Saturday nights, and asked if I was interested. The pay felt lucrative—$800 per month. Coincidentally, that was the exact amount of my rent. This sounds like God was intervening here and maybe He was. But if He was, it was to make a point, not help me with my rent.

I pondered the idea, reluctantly, but not for long. I kept thinking how wonderful it would be to take the pressure off and not worry if I could pay all my bills. I accepted their offer the next day. My first day was Sunday for training.

I arrived at the bowling alley a few minutes before I was scheduled to start just to familiarize myself with the surroundings. Everyone seemed nice enough, and the place wasn't too crowded. I had bartended before, so I wasn't starting from scratch. The place was smoky; I had forgotten about that part of bartending. I don't like inhaling second-hand smoke, and I knew I would stink like an ashtray after each shift. But it was money, right?

My training went smoothly, and it didn't take long for me to fit right in, making drinks, conversing with the customers sitting at the bar and cleaning tables. There were no surprises that night, so my trainer thought I was ready to be on my own. I was scheduled to work the following Saturday evening. It wasn't a great job, but I was going to be making the money I desperately needed to help pay the bills. At least, that was the plan.

I arrived that Saturday evening ready to go. I wanted to do a good job and make good money. The dress code was open, so I dressed appropriately, a little sexy, but not seductive. After all, I only wanted to make good tips not get hit on by guys who've had too much to drink.

After about an hour, the bar started filling up. It was a typical crowd. I had seen it all before, so this was nothing new. As the night wore on, there were a few men sitting at the bar who had been drinking at a steady pace. Getting drunk seemed to be their goal, and they were succeeding. Unfortunately, they were also heavy smokers, and I was constantly emptying their ashtrays, which disgusted me.

Then it started. At first, it was just a few dirty remarks. However, it amped up quickly to them leaning over the bar to grab at me. Even worse, to me, was the staring. Whatever they were imagining, it wasn't good. This was, by far, the worst part. These things went on for the last hour of my shift, and by the time it was over and the bar was closed, I remember thinking, "What in the world am I doing here?" I drove home that night at 1:30 a.m., exhausted, stinky from the smoke, and crying about the abuse I had just experienced. But I had $200. I looked at the money and asked myself, "Really, was it worth it?" The answer was no!

After I got home, I immediately took a shower to get the smell off me, but washing wouldn't take away the abuse. I went to the kitchen for a snack after showering, and I just lost it. I stood in the middle of my kitchen, looked up to the heavens, and started crying again asking God to help me. I asked Him to show me what I should do. I told Him I needed the money, but didn't want to go back there.

Then, my body froze. I was unable to move my body at all. It was as if I was in a trance or something. I stood there, with the feeling that something was coming over me, starting at the top of my head and moving all the way down my body. It was a tingling, yet soothing feeling, and it must have lasted a few minutes, or at least it felt that way. When it reached my feet, I heard a voice in my head say, "Get up tomorrow morning, call the owners of the bar and quit, and never step foot in that place again." The relief I felt was unbelievable, and I was able to move my body again. At that moment, I knew the Holy Spirit had descended upon me, and God had spoken to me. I collapsed in bed, exhausted.

I awoke the next morning and did exactly what God had told me to do; I quit my bartending job. I felt a huge weight removed from my shoulders. I was going to trust God with my money issues; He delivered!

Two weeks after I quit, I received an unexpected phone call from a person at the Social Security office. She explained that my first husband, my daughter's father, had applied for Social Security benefits because of a disability. Because of our daughter's age, she was entitled to $750 a month through her father's Social Security income. This would be a monthly check sent to me to help cover our daughter's expenses! I almost fainted. I just stood staring at the phone in amazement. Two weeks earlier, I quit my second job, where I would have been making about $800 a month, and, instead, trusted the Lord to provide in some way for my daughter and me. Now I learn I'm going to receive a check for $750 every month.

God is amazing, forgiving, trustworthy, and full of grace and mercy. I obeyed what He said, and by trusting Him, He was faithful and provided. This shows us His unconditional love for us. We may be broken sinners, but He will still take care of us, not because we deserve it, but because He died on the cross for our sins! He wants us to come to Him to know Him and His great love for us. What a lesson I had learned, one I will never forget!

## The Pain

Sometimes we will make good choices, and sometimes we make bad choices. This is inevitable, but as we go through our life, our dependence on God will grow, and we will trust Him to show us the right choices to make. We are all a "work in progress" until we meet our Savior someday for eternity. Until then, we must learn that God always knows what is best for us and walk in His ways, not ours. As we stumble through life, we have one constant truth: to honor a God who never changes and who loves us unconditionally regardless of our sins. We grow closer to him through prayer, studying his Word and repentance. Yet, we live in a fallen world, and sin is around every corner. Everyone struggles with the "things" of this world, and I am certainly no exception.

Even after God showed me his faithfulness when I obeyed Him, I still strayed away from Him more times that I'd like to admit. After my divorce was final, my daughter and I moved back into our home. I assumed things would start looking up for me. God had other plans, which included bringing me "down to my knees" to get my attention.

After the end of my second marriage, I was having a good time, dating, partying, and just kind of going crazy! Even my girlfriends were asking, "What is wrong with her?" I ignored everyone who told me I should stop, and I ignored God. Well, I ignored Him at least until the morning when I couldn't get out of bed. God did what he needed to do that day to get my attention. I had fallen far away from Him. I was headed into a downward spiral. I was running away from God instead of running toward Him.

I had been experiencing a shooting pain down my leg for months. I was still fitness-training clients every day, and I ignored this clear injury warning sign. I figured it would go away eventually, but it never did. Then came "that morning" when I woke up in severe pain and couldn't get up. I lay in bed crying and wondering what I was going to do. I had clients to train that day and couldn't afford to miss any work.

I rolled onto my side and reached for the nightstand to help me get out of bed. The pain was excruciating. I made my way to the dresser, and I still couldn't straighten up. I cried and cried.

I was in such pain and so distraught about my situation that I couldn't move another inch. I stood there, not knowing what to do. I couldn't call anyone; I didn't have my phone nearby. That is when God began humbling me. Looking back now, I thank the good Lord He cared enough about me to take me to that point in my life. I was a strong, independent, healthy woman, (or so I thought), but that morning I felt more like a 100-year-old woman.

I eventually was able to stand up straight enough to slowly, and ever so slowly, walk into the other room to get my phone. I first called my clients and canceled all of them, and then called a chiropractor I knew to see if he could get me in that day. I had no idea if I would even be able to drive myself there. Then I sat down in a chair, again very slowly because of the intense pain, and began looking up to the heavens. Isn't it amazing how we can just go through life ignoring God, thinking we're so good, and then when things get bad enough, we want to call on Him to fix us! How sad this must make our Heavenly Father, who so desperately wants a daily relationship with us. God is amazing and so forgiving of our faults. Praise God for that!

I prayed that morning and asked God to show me what I needed to do. I somehow knew in my heart that He was there with me and would speak to me. It calmed my inner soul, and I felt a peacefulness come over me. I did make it to the chiropractor that day, but the pain persisted for days. I slowly got better, but the pain was still there. The physical pain was joined by a pain in my soul, which was longing for something more. Despite both pains, I made the decision to "walk it off" on a nearby biking and walking trail. On that day, my true repentance and walk with the Lord began. I walked on that trail, at a slow pace, for an hour, crying the whole time. I told the Lord that I was tired of living life my way. I couldn't go on anymore as I had been and that I was turning my life over to Him. I was going to give up the sinful desires of my heart and turn toward His desires for me. I told Him he had me, and I was at the bottom of my pit. I expressed how sorry I was for not listening to Him. I poured myself out to Him desperate for Him to hear and forgive me. I promised Him that I would start living my life differently, with Him at the center. I would turn from the temptations that surrounded me. I would consistently go to church and begin reading my Bible. I asked Him to be with me, to guide me and help me through this change. I left the trail that day with new hope in my soul and a new lease on life with God at the center.

*Even to your old age and gray hairs I am he,*
*I am he who will sustain you.*
*I have made you and I will carry you;*
*I will sustain you and I will rescue you.*
Isaiah 46:4

During the next few months, I did exactly what I told the Lord I would do. I ended relationships with certain friends whom I knew were not good for me. I stayed home on weekends to resist temptations to party, and I attended church every Sunday. I adopted a kitten to keep me company on those lonely weekends alone while watching movies. This wasn't at all easy for me. I cried many times but knew that this was what was best for me. I had to deny my old life and give up all the things that kept me separated from God. I also started praying more. God began to speak to me and heal my back during this time. I felt more at peace than I had in my entire life. I knew I was doing the right things, and learning how to resist the pull of the world. I was lonely a lot at first, but was aware that God was with me all the time. At that time in my life, He was the only best friend I needed.

## Jonah

When I look back at my life so far, I realize I was always trying to run from God. If I felt a "nudging" from God, I usually chose, at least at first, to ignore it and pretend it wasn't there. I didn't want to face the fact that God might be telling me to do something differently in my life. I was fearful, and running away seemed easier. This reminds me of the story of Jonah and the Great Fish.

Jonah had heard from the Lord, but like a lot of us, he didn't like what the Lord told him to do. He was told to go to Nineveh and preach against the wickedness that had overtaken the city. Jonah, instead, ran away from the Lord toward Tarshish. He did this even though he knew "God sees all" and would know what Jonah was doing. This didn't matter to Jonah for all he wanted was to hide from the Lord. He found a ship bound for Tarshish, paid his fare, and boarded. The Lord was displeased with Jonah's disobedience, and stirred up a great wind and violent storm, which threatened to capsize the ship. The sailors were afraid and began casting cargo overboard to lighten the load of the ship.

Jonah had gone down below earlier and fell fast asleep. He didn't even know what was going on. The captain went down to wake him and asked Jonah to call on his God to help them. Even though Jonah knew that God's anger at him was the reason for the storm, he wasn't going to admit it. Eventually, Jonah's good heart won out. He feared for his life, but feared more for the unsuspecting sailors who clung terrified to their rolling ship. Jonah finally told the sailors to throw him overboard to calm the sea. He assured them they would be safe. I am sure that Jonah felt sheepish and ashamed with his attempt to hide from the Lord, especially since he had put so many others in danger.

*Nothing in all creation is hidden from God's sight.*
*Everything is uncovered and laid bare before the*
*eyes of him to whom we must give account.*
Hebrews 4:13

As I look back on my life, I can see the times I felt God leading me one way but I turned a different way. I painfully see the hurt I caused people whom I loved. I see it all and know, with a heavy heart, it could have been avoided if I had only listened to a God who knows what is best for me.

The sailors complied with Jonah's wish and threw him overboard. Immediately, the seas calmed, and the sailors rejoiced. Jonah was left swirling in the sea, not knowing what would become of him. Suddenly, a huge great fish swallowed him. Jonah was scared, but concluded being swallowed by a great fish wasn't too bad. It was at least better than drowning in the sea. He lived in the great fish for three days before his pride crumbled. He cried to the Lord in repentance for what he had done and vowed that he would make it right. This pleased God, so He had the great fish deposit Jonah onto dry land.

God knows how long to keep us in a "pit" until we come around. He is willing to give us a second chance. Praise the Lord for his compassion! The Lord again instructed Jonah to preach in the city of Nineveh. This time, Jonah obeyed. He traveled many miles to reach this large city. He walked around Nineveh for three days declaring that God would overthrow the city in forty days if the Ninevites did not change their hearts and evil ways.

To Jonah's surprise, they listened and declared a fast for all the people. Even the king took off his royal robes and covered himself with sackcloth. He issued a proclamation for repentance so that the people of Nineveh might be spared from God's fierce anger. When God saw how the Ninevites turned from their evil ways, he relented and did not bring destruction upon them.

God's reaction made Jonah angry. He couldn't understand how God could forgive them and let them live. In fact, he was so angry he asked the Lord to take his life. The Lord replied, "Is it right for you to be angry?" After all, God wanted more than 120,000 people to repent and be saved. Punishing them was a last resort. Jonah's mission was to convey God's message, which he did. God's compassion, upon seeing the Ninevites complying and repenting, led to victory for many people. Yet, Jonah wasn't happy despite the fact he did exactly as God requested. Why couldn't Jonah simply be happy?

Jonah was aware of the sins of the Ninevites. He believed they should be punished for what they were doing, not forgiven. He didn't want God to be too lenient on them and would rather have seen them suffer. Obviously, Jonah had already forgotten how the Lord forgave him of his sins, including running away from the calling of the Lord.

How does this relate to our lives? We want God to forgive us for our sins, but surely, He shouldn't forgive someone else whose sin is much worse than ours! That person should be punished for what he did, and even more so if he has offended us. We want forgiveness from others, but find it hard to forgive others when they have wronged us. Jesus died on the cross so that each one of us could be forgiven, not just some of us. The Lord will forgive someone of his sins, if he truly repents and accepts Jesus as his Savior. This applies whether the person is taking his last breath or has served the Lord his entire life. God's grace leads to eternity with the Lord. We should rejoice in this so that more may be saved to spend eternity with God. Jonah finally understood what the Lord was showing him and did rejoice in the end.

## POINTS TO PONDER

In our lives, we have choices, and we must decide the right path to take daily. Worldly influences will bombard us, and if we do not stand firm in our faith, we will fall back. When you are faced with a decision, use the following checklist to determine your resolve and intent:

- Is your decision based on God's truth? If so, what other choices in your life need to be changed to follow God's word?

- Are you trusting God to provide? How has God proven to be faithful in the past?

- Are you running from a problem or facing it? Why do you think it is hard for you to face problems head on?

- Has God had to "get your attention" about an issue? What was your response and how did you handle it?

Taking the time to ask yourself these questions is vitally important to your walk with the Lord and how you will continue to live your life. Ask God to help you make the right choices based on his word.

*But seek first his kingdom and his righteousness,*
*and all these things will be given to you as well.*
Matthew 6:33

CHAPTER FOUR

# Looking for Love, Colorado, and Hebrews

I was beginning to seek God more and really wanted to know what His answers were for my life. So, even though I had two failed marriages behind me, I wanted God to bring a man into my life I could love unconditionally, and who loved the Lord.

I began praying about this man. I asked the Lord to provide someone who was considerate, a gentleman, who loved God, enjoyed the same hobbies I did, especially physical activities, and who would treat me like a lady. I then continued, "Oh yeah, and God, could you make him tall, around my age or younger, and could he have a nice butt?" Should I really care if he was tall, my age, or had a nice rear? No! But it seemed OK to ask anyway. Thank goodness, God has a sense of humor.

A couple of months passed and some friends asked me to ride in the MS 150. This 150-mile bike ride is a fundraiser for multiple sclerosis. I wasn't sure if my back was up for the challenge, but I had been sitting around all summer. Besides, fall was approaching and I wanted to do something fun and outside. I agreed and did the ride. I had met a guy that weekend who was also riding. He seemed nice, around my age, well built, and .... We went on a few dates, and I knew he wasn't the man I had asked for from God! He had someone else in store for me, someone so much better suited for me, because God always knows what is best for us.

Sure enough, two weeks later, I met John at a winery. He had walked up to my friend and me and asked us if we would like to join him and his friends at their table. He seemed nice enough, and we moved to their table. John began talking with me and asked if he could call me sometime. I wasn't sure about him yet, but decided to give him my phone number anyway. He called me a few days later and asked me to go to a baseball game, which I declined. I wanted to be sure God was in on this one, so I was taking it slowly.

The next Saturday came, and my friend talked me into going back to the same winery that afternoon. I normally wouldn't have gone, but she seemed desperate to go, so I agreed to it. Once again, John was there, too. He spotted me sitting at a table, and he came over to say hi. He was polite and asked if he could sit down and talk with me. I couldn't turn him down. He seemed so nice and was rather handsome, so we chatted for the next hour or so. Then, I will never forget John's opening line to ask me on another date.

He said, "Would you like to hike the Grand Canyon?" How about that for a first date? That was sure better than a ballgame. I loved hiking and thought it would be a fun adventure. We agreed to meet for a drink later to discuss the possibilities of a Grand Canyon hike. I realized that John was a real sweetheart, polite, kind, a complete gentleman. He also had a big heart. I started to think that maybe he was the man God had sent into my life. We began dating regularly, but there were two things that bothered me; his age, and he didn't talk about the Lord.

When I first met John, I was a little hesitant. He met all the "criteria" I had given God, but I was concerned about his age. He was twelve years older than me, and I had no idea where he stood regarding faith. Now wait a minute, those were two biggies for me. For some reason, I struggled with the age thing, but God worked on me, and I got over it. I had to ask John about the Lord, though. This subject was truly the most important thing to me. So we talked, and he agreed to go to church with me on Sundays.

We slowly became more involved in our church and even began reading and discussing the Bible together. We continued dating and even talked about getting married. He was a wonderful man with a big, generous heart. God was changing both of us, slowly but surely turning our hearts more toward Him. We still were not doing things completely God's way in our relationship, and I felt the need to rectify that. On the night before John was leaving on his first mission trip to Guatemala, I approached him with my request. I told him that if wanted to get married, we would have to do things

God's way. Everything in our relationship needed to be pure, which meant we had to stop having intimate relations with each other. He quickly agreed and we vowed to each other, and God, that we would begin this transformation right then. And we did! I'll never forget that night, June 25, when we completely devoted ourselves to our Loving Father. It wasn't easy; we had been dating for almost two years, and things were going to be different than before. John was an absolute gentleman and never went back on his word. I knew he loved me, and he also loved God! We were on this journey together and looked forward to seeing God working in our lives. We did hike the Grand Canyon about one year into our relationship, and it was an unforgettable experience. It's amazing how God works things out!

## Colorado

John and I are avid hikers, so we planned another trip to Colorado to walk new paths together there. We loved exploring in nature, and this particular trip turned out to be quite an experience. We began our trip in Ouray, a beautiful valley town that exudes charm and peacefulness.

Our next stop was Silverton, Colorado, a tiny town with its history based in an old silver mining camp. The year-round population is a whopping 600 inhabitants. It consisted of four square miles that held one small hotel/B&B, where we stayed, a couple of greasy spoon cafes, one gas station, and a few gift shops. Quaint is the perfect word to describe Silverton. As we parked the car, I laughed and said our dinner would probably be at one of the greasy spoons eating some good old country food, not our usual fare. We decided to take our hike first instead of checking into our hotel right then.

After hiking about three and one-half hours, and as we neared the end of our trail, I said to John, "I am starving! Wouldn't it be great to be able to sit down to a five-course dinner with a glass of wine and some yummy dessert for our meal this evening?" We both laughed, knowing that our dinner would be at one of the cafes in town. Little did we suspect God had other ideas.

As we checked into our hotel, a man wearing chef's attire appeared through a doorway at the back of the hotel. He strolled through the hallway toward us and asked if we would be joining in the dinner for that evening. We were both taken aback. John and I looked at each other and, after a few moments, asked what he meant. He explained he was a five-star chef, and that he would be serving a seven-course meal that evening in a small candlelit dining room complete with wine and dessert! We had no idea this hotel even served food as it wasn't mentioned in the literature. I wanted someone to pinch me because it seemed so surreal. We finally answered him in unison, "Of course we will be joining you for dinner!"

We could not believe our good fortune, nor could we give any logical explanation for what had just happened. Did God hear the words I had spoken while coming down the mountain about the five-course dinner? That would be so like God—deliver something to us that seems utterly impossible. **John and I do believe that God**

**was showing us that He hears what we say and knows what we are thinking.** We also believe He enjoys performing "miracles" even in our present day world. Absolutely, God can do anything!

*For you are great and do marvelous deeds;*
*you alone are God.*
Psalm 86:10

Only God could have arranged the scenario that day and made it work out the way it did down to every detail. I am still in awe every single time that God Speaks to me! Thank you, God, for an absolutely wonderful dinner and lovely breakfast the next morning. What an unexpected blessing!

This reminds me of the Bible story of Sarah. She laughed at God when the angel told her she would bear a child in her old age. She assumed it could never happen because the circumstances were not right. She was past her childbearing years—way past. But she forgot that God could accomplish anything He wants no matter what the so-called "circumstances" are. In fact, in the unexpected is where God shows us His Power best. These stories teach us to have more faith and trust in our Almighty God for whatever we need or want. He loves to bless us because we are His children.

## Hebrews

In September, John and I joined a Bible study at our church. After we returned home from the first meeting, I was drawn to continue reading my Bible that night. For some reason, the book of Hebrews caught my attention. I was reading while lying on my bed. I grew so comfortable that I became sleepy. I considered getting up to sit in a chair, but dismissed that idea. The next thing I knew, my bedroom light flickered on and off a couple of times, which had never happened before. I felt like God was telling me to get up and keep reading. So I did. I moved into the kitchen to continue reading, and I read the entire book of Hebrews that night. I learned a lot, and even cried as I felt God speaking to me through his Word. But it was the last scripture in the book that almost knocked me off my chair. Hebrews 13:24 reads, "Greet all your leaders and all God's people. Those from Italy send you their greetings." This was significant in that moment because John and I were leaving for Italy in two days! Who would have thought the word Italy would appear in the Bible—certainly not me. I sat there dumbfounded, crying. I knew God was speaking to me. He was letting me know that He knew everything about me, and that He was right there with me. I believe He was showing me how intimate He could be with me. I felt so loved by God; it was overwhelming! He guided me to read the book of Hebrews that night so He could speak to me—unbelievable. Who was I that God cared that much about me? Why would He take time out from all the people in the world to speak to me? I couldn't wrap my mind around it, but I knew how incredibly good it made me feel.

*...in these last days he has spoken to us by his Son,*
*whom he appointed heir of all things, and through*
*whom he made the universe.*

Hebrews 1:2

God loves every one of us that much and He wants to speak to us every day; we just have to be willing to listen and patiently wait. We have to be willing to read His Word, meditate on it, and do what it says. God wants a relationship with each person. We are important to Him. He treasures us as His children, and we are all His children. When God knows you are serious about your relationship with Him, He will speak to you; never doubt that, He is willing and ready.

## POINTS TO PONDER

"God knows all" is a good place to start. He is all-seeing, all-knowing, and all-hearing. He knows everything we think, feel, speak, and want. So why do we have a hard time believing this? Next time you need something, try these things:

- Pray about a particular need you have. How did God answer that prayer?

- Patiently wait to hear the answer. When was the last time you waited on an answer?

- Be obedient when God shows you the answer. How did that obedience change the outcome?

- Thank Him for the outcome. How does having a thankful heart affect your attitude?

Write down a prayer for a particular need you have right now and then wait on the Lord to answer it.

*In the beginning,*
*God created the heavens and the earth.*

Genesis 1:1

*God saw all that he had made,*
*and it was very good.*

Genesis 1:31

CHAPTER FIVE

# Italy Biking, England Hiking and the Moving Sale

Going to Italy had always been a dream of mine, and John and I made that dream come true. The trip was a six-day journey, by bike, across the Tuscany region. We were so excited and had trained hard for the twenty-five to forty miles per day of biking. Neither one of us had ever done anything like that before. We weren't sure what to expect, but we knew it would be an adventure!

We stayed in numerous locations and in different venues; some were hotels, but one was an old monastery. A van moved our luggage from place to place; all we had to worry about was staying upright on our bikes and moving forward.

Our adventure began in Rome, where we stayed one day and night. John likes to hit the ground running. Since he had been to Rome before, he wanted to share as many sights as possible with me. By the time afternoon rolled around, I was ready for a nap, which he abruptly told me I was not allowed to take. He said I had to wait until bedtime that evening so I could get back on a normal sleep schedule. I told him—in a loving way, of course—that if I didn't get a nap soon, I would not be responsible for what might happen to him! I was able to take a nap, and we enjoyed the rest of our evening strolling around the streets of Rome and dining in a quaint cafe. The next morning, we headed to Montecatini Terme to meet our Tuscany bike tour group.

The bike tour took us into the most beautiful parts of Italy including Florence and Venice. The days flew by, and it was so joyful to be spending time with John in this way. Before we knew it, the six days were over, and our time in Italy was ending. While I hated for it to end, I was excited about our next stop—England. John had arranged for us to stay in Amberley Castle for three nights. He did this for me. Once he realized how much I loved castles, he made a point of making sure I was able to experience it firsthand.

## England Hiking

So off we went from Venice, by cab, water boat, train, cab, and plane to England. We rented a car to get to the castle. What a trip that all was. The first sighting of the castle was breathtaking. It was grand, beautiful, elegant, and medieval-looking all at once. I couldn't help but stand there and stare at it. It looked just like the pictures I had seen, but even more massive and stately than I could have imagined. We walked around the grounds and enjoyed a glass of wine in the bar before checking into our room.

The room was equally as gorgeous dripping with dark red and green fabrics and wall coverings. The ornate wooden bed frame was covered in beautiful carvings. Everything was elegant and romantic, but we were still keeping our vow to God to remain pure. That meant sleeping on opposite sides of the bed fully clothed. It wasn't quite as romantic as one would expect, especially in a castle! We promised, however, and we intended on keeping our promise. We both slept well that night and woke to a beautiful morning in the English countryside.

We had decided to visit Arundel Castle about five miles away. We elected to hike the distance versus driving to experience England close up. Our walk took us across lush, rolling farmland. We asked a local for directions. We were instructed to walk along a raised dirt path between a quick-flowing river and a farmer's field of cows. When we started out, there was a mist in the air, along with a little nip, typical of England's weather. I was walking ahead of John on the path. We walked in silence for a while absorbing the quietness of the country.

The quiet was suddenly pierced by a loud sad-sounding cow call. Startled, I turned to see John making the distressing noise. He laughed when I asked him what he was doing and made the "call" again. He did this at least five times, very loudly. The cows responded by walking toward us. There must have been a whole herd of 100 to 150 cows. Normally, having a herd of cows approaching me probably wouldn't bother me too much, but the only thing separating them from us was a rickety wooden fence. Even this knowledge wouldn't have bothered me, except the cows weren't leisurely walking toward us; they were running. If the fence was knocked over, the only thing between us and a herd of excited cows was the quick-flowing, muddy, cold river.

Concerned, I turned around to say something to John. His face was white as a sheet, and his eyes were opened wide. I had a bad feeling that we were possibly in a lot of trouble. All he said was "Walk faster." I turned back around and started to jog, not knowing what was about to happen or how we might get out of the situation. I shouldn't have worried; God intervened. Out of nowhere, two quail flew out of a small bush near the fence. They fluttered and flapped around making quite a bit of noise for two small birds. Then, they soared into the sky. Immediately, every one of those cows stopped dead in its tracks. The entire herd put the brakes on and didn't move. It was the strangest thing. They just stood there for several seconds. Then, almost as if they had just awakened, one-by-one they turned and walked toward the field where they were before.

John and I stood staring at the retreating cows in amazement. What had just happened? We couldn't believe that two small quail would have such an impact on a herd of cows. We agreed it was one of God's small miracles, and we thanked Him for his perfect timing and his protection. We knew He was right there with us, keeping us safe. God loves to perform miraculous things for us so that we understand He can do anything!

*I guide you in the way of wisdom and lead you*
*along straight paths. When you walk,*
*your steps will not be hampered;*
*when you run, you will not stumble.*
Proverbs 4:11-12

His power is absolute, and He loves for us to give him our praise! After we both recovered from the calamity, I asked John what he was thinking about doing when the cows were stampeding. He told me he was going to grab my hand and jump into the river! I would have cried if he had done that. The river was cold, muddy and moving fast. Who knows what would have happened to us in that current. I suppose God knew he needed to intervene quickly before John threw me in the river. I praised God even more for his perfect timing after hearing John's solution. I later asked him what his silly cow call had communicated to the cows. He nonchalantly replied, "Oh, it was a distressed calf call. It signals the adult cows that a calf is hurt." I (gently) punched him on the arm for that.

We arrived at Arundel Castle in one piece, took the tour, and took the train back to Amberley Castle instead of walking back. No sense in giving John the opportunity to do more mischief. Little did

I know, he had some fun and, dare I say, romantic mischief in mind over dinner.

That night we were going to have dinner in the castle restaurant, and John seemed nervous. I wasn't sure why and when I asked him he said it was nothing. We had a lovely dinner by candlelight. It was very romantic. I ordered ice cream for dessert. The waiter delivered it with a flourish. Amused, I put my spoon in and promptly hit something hard. I told John that there was something in my ice cream bowl. I started digging around and found a large hard plastic purple ring, the kind a parent would buy a child. I dug it out and wiped it off, laughing. John took this opportunity to get down on one knee, take my hand, and ask me to marry him. I was laughing so hard that he had to ask me three times before I could say yes. He put the purple ring on my finger and showed me that it could light up red, too! We were both laughing and savoring the moment.

God knew exactly what he was doing when he arranged for John and me to meet those two years before. Thank goodness, I trusted the Lord. I proudly wore that purple ring as my engagement ring for a couple of months until we were married. I really love that man. He is so much fun; life is a real adventure with him.

## THE MOVING SALE

We decided to keep our wedding plans simple by only inviting family. We set the date for the end of November. That meant we only had a little over two months to pull it together. Even with keeping it simple, there were many things to do: choose a location, decide on the reception menu, and find a beautiful, but budget-conscious, wedding dress! It was an exciting time that brought with it many changes, including the decision of what to do with our houses. We both owned our homes, and we were still living apart.

We decided to sell both of our homes and buy one together to be able to start fresh. It was important to us to begin our new life together in a new place. We also decided that I would move into his home after we were married, leaving my home for the time being, since his home was quite a bit larger.

On a crisp, early November day, we were biking through neighborhoods. We rode past a "for sale" sign pointing down a side street. I was in front of John and something made me take a sharp turn and head down this street. John followed, and there it was—The House! It was a lovely older home with a beautiful yard and a white picket fence. I stopped my bike and just stood there staring at it. It couldn't have been more perfect, at least on the outside, but I was sure the inside would be just as lovely.

As we stood there staring, a man from across the street walked over, told us he was a real estate broker, and said he had a key if we wanted to see the inside. He let us in to look around. It had so much character. John and I agreed this was our house. The buying process went smoothly and quickly. The next step was to put John's house on the market and get married. The wedding came off beautifully, and our honeymoon was amazing and memorable. We were both so incredibly happy.

The wedding was over, and the December holidays came and went. We had put John's house up for sale in November, but it hadn't sold yet. We hadn't moved into our new home because we had decided to do some remodeling. With it being winter, we assumed his house wouldn't sell quickly. God, of course, had other plans. The house sold in early January, and the new owners wanted immediate possession.

With the new home still being remodeled, John and I moved back to my small home and put the majority of his belongings into storage. While it wasn't fun, we were grateful his house had sold. The next step was to pare down our respective possessions because they wouldn't all fit in the new place. We decided to hold a moving sale at my house once we were settled in our new home.

The sale day was over Memorial Day weekend. There wasn't one empty space in my old house. Every nook and cranny had something to sell: furniture, kitchen appliances, pictures, area rugs, outdoor items, and so much more!

One night before the sale, we decided to give whatever money was made to our church to be used for mission work and the homeless ministry. We felt so blessed by God; we wanted to help with these efforts and felt led by God to do so.

The signs for the sale stated that all the money would go to charity. A few of our friends at church volunteered to help us at the sale. We all prayed that a lot of money would be raised and that there would be a steady stream of people coming to our sale.

The day arrived; we opened for business promptly at 7:00 a.m. People were waiting to get in, and the flow didn't stop until we closed the door in the afternoon. We were tired, but happy so much had sold. We decided to count the money before leaving after a friend asked to see how much was made for the church ministries.

It took us twenty minutes to get the total: $3,350. We couldn't believe it! We were thrilled. John and I thanked God for such a wonderful day of serving Him as we drove home that night.

Later that night, I was awakened by the telephone. I almost didn't answer it. I did mainly because I was concerned that someone was calling us at such a late hour. The caller was my mother. I sat up, expecting bad news. Instead, she said quite happily, "What are you doing?" I said, "Sleeping, or trying to, what's up?" She continued, "Well, do you remember two months ago when I asked you and John and your sister to go in with us on a raffle ticket at our church?" I had a vague memory of agreeing to this. "Well, tonight was the drawing at our parish picnic, and we won!" She continued, "Do you want to know what your share of it is?" I managed to mumble, "Sure what is it?" She dropped the bomb that John and I had won $3,333! I wasn't sure I heard her right. I repeated the number, and she assured me that I was correct. I thanked her for calling me, said good-bye, and then laid next to a still-sleeping John thinking about it. Then, it hit me like a lightning bolt. At the sale, we had raised $3,350 for the missions at our church, and God had just given us a gift of $3,333!

*From the fullness of his grace we have all received*
*one blessing after another.*
John 1:16

I was in awe and amazement at what our Heavenly Father had done! I woke John up to tell him the news. God had blessed us. He was showing us that His Word is Truth, that when you give to others, He will reward you tenfold in some way for your faithfulness. It took a while to fall back to sleep, but when I awoke in the morning, there was praise on my lips to our wonderful Savior!

## POINTS TO PONDER

Whether we are traveling around the world or in our own home, our Heavenly Father is always there ready to bless us. He shows us his love because He is love; always and forever. He knows us intimately and wants to show us that in every aspect of our lives.

- Have you felt his presence lately? In what ways do you feel his nearness to you?

- Do you count your blessings every day? How does that help you in your daily life?

- Have you witnessed his help even when you didn't ask for it? How has that helped to change your dependence on Him?

- Do you sense his unconditional love for you? Who in your life do you need to love "unconditionally"?

As you ask yourself these questions, try to imagine how much God loves you and cares for you.

*Do not be anxious about anything, but in every-*
*thing, by prayer and petition, with thanksgiving,*
*present your requests to God. And the peace of*
*God, which transcends all understanding, will*
*guard your hearts and minds in Christ Jesus.*
Philippians 4:6-7

CHAPTER SIX

# A God-Appointed Meeting, Mexico, and the Van

The moving sale quickly became a memory. Our focus became the sale of my house. We were ready to own just one home! What God did in the midst of selling this home is truly an amazing testimony of how our Lord can comfort others through us.

John and I worked feverishly to get my home ready to be sold. We emptied it, cleaned it, restored floors, and shampooed carpets. There was some haste to getting the house ready because we decided to sell it ourselves and had advertised our first open house. It was a hot, sunny July day, and we had no idea how many people would show up. We had a few people stop by through the afternoon, but no one seemed to be too interested at the time. As 4:00 p.m. approached, a car pulled in the driveway. Even though I was ready to go home, I graciously greeted the couple and showed them in. They were thrilled with how the house looked, loved the location, and truly seemed interested in it. The woman asked if she could see the deck and the backyard, so I opened the sliding door for her and went out with her.

My house sat on about one-half acre. As she looked around, she proceeded to tell me about a house they used to own which she missed very much. She asked me if I knew where Faith Lutheran Church was. Her question gave me a chill because that was where we went to church. She said they used to own the house behind the church. I told her that Faith Lutheran was using their former home as a storage facility for the "homeless ministry." I also shared that I had been in it a couple of times, the most recent being that morning. She looked surprised, and asked what it looked like inside. "It's still set up like a house," I answered. I described what I saw when I walked into the kitchen, basement, and bedrooms earlier that day. We both remarked how amazing it was that I had actually been in that home on this very day. She fell silent as if she was contemplating something. "Is there still a child's bedroom in the home?" Her question was barely finished, and I knew that this was the work of our Heavenly Father. Only God could have orchestrated our meeting. I moved a little closer to her and said, "Yes, there is still a child's room there. In fact, I was drawn to that room." I explained how I stood in that quiet space looking at the paintings of bears and children's sayings painted on the walls. I wondered about the child who had lived in this bedroom. I stood transfixed with an extraordinary feeling of peace surrounding and flowing through me. It was very strange, to say the least. As I left the room, I knew God must be up to something. There was no other explanation as to why I had been so drawn to that room.

She began to cry as I described my feelings while in the room. Through her tears, she shared how she lost her six-week-old son to SIDS (Sudden Infant Death Syndrome) in that room. My heart fell into my feet; I was so sad for her obvious pain. I hugged her and cried with her. We were brought together in this moment for a reason, God's reason, and it was both so sweet and sorrowful. We went back into the house after we gained some composure, and she left with her husband. An hour later, she called and asked to put a contract on the house. I was so excited knowing our house would sell to this sweet couple. This must be why God had orchestrated all this! I told John, and we thanked God for his faithfulness. I learned the next day to never assume I understand God's intentions.

The next afternoon, she called me again, but this time to say they had to back out of buying my home; they just couldn't afford it. I told her not to worry about it, and I was sorry that they wouldn't be moving in. She finished our conversation with, "Above all, it was such a pleasure to meet you and to know that our house is being used for good things through your church and that my son's room is still the same. I know that God sent you to me to give me a sense of peace and contentment in my heart about my son, and for that I am truly grateful!"

I was humbled to be used by God to bring comfort to another human being. We never know what God's plans are, and they are always better than anything we could imagine. We didn't sell our house that day, but I didn't care. My experience with that still-grieving mother was worth more to me than any amount of money; I saw the Lord God, our Savior, doing his awesome work.

## Mexico

We had a couple more open houses but still no bites from anyone to buy it. In the meantime, John and I went on our second mission trip to Mexico. I had been to Matamoras, Mexico on my first mission trip the previous July. I fell in love with Matamoras and Esther who ran the orphanage there. We decided to go together, knowing God would be working to show his glory and miracles.

We arrived in Matamoras on Saturday, settled into our room, and reviewed the schedule for our stay. On Sunday, we were to visit four different churches, staying for each service. We fussed a little over having to attend four services, but realized later that God always has a plan.

We headed out Sunday morning for the first church service. We were a cheerful group of twelve people, some of whom wore the t-shirts another group member, Steve, had made for the trip. He had inscribed a Bible verse on the back. As we entered the church and took our seats, we noticed a big poster hanging on the wall with the number 254 on it. As the pastor began speaking, he referred to a scripture that they had been studying for a week now, which tied into the school bus poster. It was Psalm 25:4 —"Show me your ways, O Lord, teach me your paths..." We sat stunned. This was the exact scripture on the back of our t-shirts. What was the likelihood that Steve would choose that verse out of all the Bible verses he could have picked, not to mention it happened to be the same one at the church in Mexico? That would have been a big coincidence, but since we know there are no coincidences when it comes to God, we knew the Lord Almighty had planned that one. Once again, God showed us that He will direct our path. Praise be to Him who knows all things! After that display from God, we graciously sat through all the other church services that day and never uttered a cross or impatient word.

A few days later, I felt this "nudge" to ask Steve Smith, who was in charge of the group, if the women could take some food to the orphanage. He thought this was a great idea. We loaded up the van with as much as we could carry, knowing that the orphanage was home to about thirty-nine very hungry children!

Esther, the woman who started the home for these orphaned kids, met us at the door. She was surprised to see us, having had no idea we were coming. When we opened the van doors, and she saw all the food we had brought, she began crying. We learned she had been praying for two days for God to send someone with food to the orphanage because they really needed it. Her faith was inspirational; she told us she never doubted that God would deliver what she was praying for. This is how she approached everything in her life, praying and trusting God to answer those prayers.

*Now faith is being sure of what we hope for and*
*certain of what we do not see.*
Hebrews 11:1

There was no food to be found in the orphanage kitchen. The freezer was completely empty, and the refrigerator was nearly so. She wasn't kidding when she said they needed food desperately! I just always stand in awe of God when I see things like this unfold. Esther prayed, and God nudged my heart. We see here the connection between praying and God answering prayers. God didn't need Esther's prayers, but He wanted to get the glory for this and to show others that He always hears and will answer us, at times in unexpected ways. We unloaded all the food and played with the children for a while.

I walked to the back of the orphanage's yard toward the swing set where three little boys were playing and swinging. As I approached them, I heard them singing a song in Spanish. I stopped to listen to their sweet voices. They suddenly switched from Spanish to English. To my astonishment, it was "Open the eyes of my heart Lord." How did these little boys know English? I had never heard any children there speak English before. Why did they pick that song to sing as I walked up? We should all know the answer to that. God predestined that moment to speak to my heart and prepare me for something he was going to have John and me do for His kingdom. I began tearing up while they sang. After a bit, they switched back to Spanish. I asked the Lord to show me his plan, please. He was "opening the eyes of my heart" to know him better, to hear him better, and to share in the power of what he wanted me to do.

On our journey back to our rooms, Steve asked all of us to pray about something for Esther. She needed a passenger van to transport the children back and forth to their school in the city. Their current transportation was unsafe, time-consuming and caused the children to be late at times. As soon as Steve mentioned the van, something inside of me whispered that John and I could do that. I vowed that we would buy one as soon as my house sold.

I knew that before I said anything, I needed to talk this over with John. So after dinner, I discussed it with him. We decided that as soon as my house sold, we would buy a van for the orphanage. We prayed that night asking God to sell my house to make it possible for us to bless the orphanage with a van. Well, God had a little different plan. We learned to never give God a stipulation about giving a blessing to others. In other words, we learned we couldn't say, "God if you do this for us, then we will do this for you!" That's not how God works. Yet, He can turn anything around and use it for His good purposes, which is exactly what He did.

## The Van

We returned to St. Louis with a renewed energy for selling the house. But a month passed, and the house was still ours. Meanwhile, we knew that Esther and the children still needed a van. One morning John said, "Maybe we need to just step out in faith, buy a van, and know that God will provide what we need." I agreed. Having made our decision, John set out to find a van in the local paper. It took less than ten minutes. He found the perfect vehicle, a "1997 Dodge Ram 15 passenger van for $4,995"! This is exactly what we were looking for and in the right price range.

I called the owner immediately. No one answered, so I left a message. I waited patiently all day. I received a call about 4:00 p.m. The man was nice, with a gentle voice. I asked him a few questions about the van, like what color it was (not that it mattered in the least) and what kind of shape it was in. He answered all my questions. Before I could tell him why we were interested in buying the van, he said to me, "I just need to let you know that this van had been bought originally for a senior housing nursing facility. They had changed the seating around somewhat to accommodate the elderly people who would be using it." He explained that there was an aisle placed in the center of the van, making it more like a school bus. A school bus—I couldn't believe it! I never mentioned the reason we were buying it was for children to get to school.

My excitement was short-lived, however, because someone else had called first. The owner thought the other person was going to look at it that night. My heart sank. This was the perfect vehicle for the orphanage. I needed to pray about it—hard. I actually told the man I was going to pray that the other person wouldn't show up or decide not to buy it. I started praying as soon as I hung up the phone. I prayed that if it was God's will for us to buy this van, we would get a call back that evening.

Two hours later, the phone rang; it was David, the man selling the van. He asked if we were still interested in looking at the van. He added, "It must have been a 'divine intervention,' because the other man called and said he was no longer interested in it." I assured him we were still interested and set up a time the next evening to go and take a look. As we ended our conversation, I praised God for his faithfulness and answer to our prayer.

*And we know that in all things God works for the*
*good of those who love him, who have been called*
*according to his purpose.*
Romans 8:28

When we met David, we told him our story about the orphanage as we examined the van. It was perfect, at least perfectly set up just like a school bus. Unfortunately, it did need a little bit of work done. Since some repairs were needed, we offered him $4,000, which was almost $1,000 lower than what he was asking. He accepted our offer, even though he owed $5,400 on the line of credit, and said he would contribute the extra $1,400 as his donation to the orphanage! He also offered to fix a few things and clean it up for us. God is simply amazing! Not only did He lead us to the perfect van, but he also put it on David's heart to donate his talents and treasures on behalf of the children in Mexico! How can we not praise a

God like ours? His plan is always bigger and better than anything we could possibly imagine! All we have to do is step out in faith and trust Him and his plans. He will do the rest for us, and then we can give Him all the glory.

We drove that van to Mexico in late September. That van was packed with everything from diapers to blankets to formula to clothing and anything else we could jam in. Our church had donated all the items. It was a slow trip, but when we arrived in the van to greet Esther, the look on her face and the tears of joy streaming down her cheeks were worth more than anything in this world. God spoke once again to the hearts of many along the way to accomplish his will for Esther and the children. He is an awesome God full of compassion, fulfilling the needs of his people.

Remember the house we couldn't seem to sell? Two days after buying the van, we received two phone calls about buying it. Those inquiries fell through, but we eventually sold it to a pastor and his wife. They wanted to hold weekly teenage Bible studies in the house. How blessed were we that God sold our house and used it for his glory. All I can say is, "Amen!"

## POINTS TO PONDER

God is amazing; he always provides. He ministers to others through us, he orchestrates events for his purposes, and he chooses to use us in ways where He will get the glory. Have you seen his provision in your life by...

- Experiencing peace and contentment from a friend reaching out to you? How did that make you feel—joyful, thankful, encouraged?

- Experiencing a blessing in your life from giving a blessing to another? Why do you think God likes to bless us and others?

- Receiving something that was a much needed item when it seemed impossible? What other time in your life did God come through in an "impossible" circumstance?

- Sharing a story with someone and watching God involve another person to get the job done? How else has God intervened in your life, and how did it help you?

When we place our hope and trust in the Lord, we will never be disappointed. He will always come through!

*The king was overjoyed and gave orders to lift*
*Daniel out of the den. And when Daniel was lifted*
*from the den, no wound was found on him,*
*because he had trusted in his God.*

Daniel 6:23

CHAPTER SEVEN

# Bike Accident, Fundraising Letter, and Noah

In our lives, we all have things we put our trust in: other people, bank accounts, stocks and bonds, brakes on our cars, doctors, etc. These things can all become "untrustworthy," but our God can be trusted with everything in our lives, regardless of the situation. When we learn to do this, many of our problems and frustrations melt away: and we begin to see how good God is at taking care of us. I seem to learn things the hard way, and my bike accident is one I will never forget.

It was a beautiful morning in August; the sun was shining, and there was a cool breeze. I woke up feeling energized and excited about the day. We were going to meet with a friend of ours and then work at the homeless ministry that evening. I decided since it was going to be a busy day, I would take an early morning bike ride. This was something I didn't normally do during the week because of morning traffic. But today was different; I was going to brave it. I dressed in the brightest colored jersey I had, one that I usually never wore. I wanted to be certain everyone on the road would see me.

My husband had equipped my bike (and me) with extra flashers. I now had one in the front, one in the back, and one on my back! I finally got out the door, feeling a little like a Christmas tree.

The ride was wonderful, and traffic wasn't too bad. About a half mile from home, I decided to ride in the street because a mom with two children was walking ahead of me on the sidewalk. I was singing along with my praise and worship songs on my iPod when a car turned sharply into a driveway right in front of me.

All I remember thinking was I couldn't stop and I am going to hit her car. I screamed, "Oh dear God!" I must have blacked out because the next thing I remember is hitting the pavement hard, first my butt then my elbow and head. Boom! I went down in a big way. Even though I was a little stunned by the impact, I immediately sat up. I was in the middle of the street with cars stopped all around me. My mangled bike was about six feet away. A man walked up and asked if I was OK. I nodded, and he helped me to my feet. As I stood swaying a little unsteadily, I had the strangest feeling come over me. It felt as if the Lord was speaking directly to me starting with my feet and working his way up to my head. I had the strongest sense that my body was fine; nothing was broken. An immediate sense of peace came over me.

The man who helped me up also retrieved my bike, putting it on the grass. Watching him, I realized just how far I had flown through the air! The fact I wasn't hit by another car while flying through the air and landing on the pavement was truly an amazing act of God, especially since cars were backed up in each direction because of me. The mom on the sidewalk had stopped to make a call. She yelled to me that she had called for an ambulance. I told her I was sure I was OK, but she was having none of that. She replied, "I saw the whole thing happen right in front of me. You flew a long way and landed hard. You must be really tough to not be hurt in any way." She then said an ambulance was already on the way, and I should be checked out just in case. I thanked her for her help as I walked to the sidewalk.

It was about this time the woman who had caused the accident approached me. She apologized for not seeing me. Didn't see me? I had three flashers going and the brightest colored top ever! Instead of saying that, God gave me the grace to tell her not to worry about it. I turned away and thanked God that I was fine.

After that, the ambulance and two police officers arrived. The police asked me a few questions, and the paramedics asked me if I was sure I wasn't hurt. They told me that normally when they get a call about a biker and a car colliding, the biker usually sustains many injuries that require an ambulance ride. I then told them I was fine because God had been there watching over me. One of them kind of half-grinned, and told me how lucky I was. I replied by telling them how awesome God is, and He is my protector!

John showed up with the car, and we loaded my gnarled bike into the back. Once we were home, I was able to reflect on the whole event. John and I both had tried to protect me from an accident by "human effort"—the flashers and bright top—which didn't do any good at all. We failed that morning to put our trust in the Lord and pray about my protection knowing that He is in control of everything. Psalm 5:11 says, "But let all who take refuge in you be glad; let them ever sing for joy. Spread your protection over them that those who love your name may rejoice in you." As I read those words, I was reminded of God's promises. He can be trusted with our lives. He is the one who made us, and He is faithful.

I realized something else as I changed my clothes. The bike shorts I was wearing didn't have any holes or tears in them. I wondered how that could be since I flew through the air, hit the pavement, and scraped the ground with the right side of my rear. Upon closer investigation, I discovered there wasn't even a pulled thread or abrasion in the material. I felt God speak to me right then saying He had put his hand down on the ground to catch me and break my fall. I started weeping and got on my knees to praise our awesome God. He really was watching over me and shielding me from terrible injury. This act of love toward me has strengthened my walk with the Lord, and I will be forever grateful.

## Fundraising Letter

Not too long after my bike accident, I had to put my trust in the Lord again. After one of our mission trips to Matamoras, I felt like God was calling me to help raise some funds for the orphanage. One day, I sat down at my computer and began pouring my heart out about what I had seen in Matamoras. I wrote about the poverty, about the living conditions, the lack of food and clean water, the children, etc. Here is part of my letter:

*"John and I recently returned from a mission trip to Matamoras, Mexico. The seven days that we spent there have changed our lives in an unbelievable way. We have both been on other mission trips, but what we witnessed during this stay was heart wrenching.*

*Let me begin by telling you about the fishing village devastated by the hurricane. When we arrived there, at least half of the homes had been completely destroyed. Please keep in mind that these people have little to nothing and families live in three-room shacks, if they are lucky. This is what they had taken away. Many of them had their beds outside with maybe a sheet or tarp suspended over it. Some of them had nothing. The pastor of the church had his home destroyed. He has a wife and three children. They had a makeshift home in the church with some of the other families. Food was scarce, as it always was, but now it was worse than ever..*

*On Thursday that week, the women were able to visit "The Dump." The only way to describe the "dump" is hell on earth. When we arrived, there were somewhere between 50 to 100 people literally digging through huge piles of trash just to find some small nugget of something that looked good enough to sell for a few cents so that they could buy some food; or they were looking for something good enough to eat.*

*Can you imagine digging through a trash dump looking for food? They stand in the stench (believe me, you have never smelled anything like this before) with zillions of flies swarming around them, waiting for the dump truck to unleash its treasures. They are starving—what would you do? Thank God that we were able to take some rice, beans, and bags of potatoes to hand out to some of them. Many had to be turned away because we ran out of food. That was the hardest thing to do was to close the van doors and drive away while people who had stood in line had received nothing. When you have to leave a place like this, all you can do is cry about the injustice."*

*Defend the cause of the weak and fatherless; maintain the rights of the poor and oppressed.*
Psalm 82:3

I added some pictures from our trip to the letter, so readers could see what I was writing about. The letter was finished, but I was unsure as to whether I should send it. Hurricane Katrina had just hit, and there was so much devastation and need here in the

U.S. from it. I prayed the next morning, and the Lord led me to Hosea 1:7, "Yet I will show love to the house of Judah; and I will save them—not by bow, sword or battle, or by horses and horsemen, but by the Lord their God." You see, although God asks us to do our part in this world to help others, we need to remember that He is not limited to our human effort. God chooses to work through us because it is good for us, not because He needs our help. He can accomplish all his purposes without us if he chooses to. We don't have the power or ability to disrupt or achieve anything that God has planned to do!

I realized the depth of this scripture and knew I needed to be obedient and send the letter. I promised to trust God to take care of the rest. He was using me to help accomplish something He wanted to do. It was a blessing for me to be used by God for His work. I made one hundred copies of the letter and pulled together my list of names and addresses.

Within a couple of days, I was ready for the mass mailing. I said a prayer as I mailed them and knew that God would take it from there. The response was unbelievable. In three short weeks, we received many donations: one for $5,000, one for $1,000, and several for smaller amounts. In total, that letter brought in $13,500. All the glory goes to God, for it was His Power that accomplished this. He used me to write a simple letter from the heart to get done what He wanted. We never know what stepping out in obedience is going to accomplish for the Lord's kingdom until we do it. We have to be obedient to that "still, small voice" in our heads and not doubt, but trust that God knows what He is doing.

## Noah

A Bible story that perfectly illustrates this idea is Noah and the Ark. I can't imagine what Noah thought when God called him to build an ark. First, he didn't live anywhere near any water; it hadn't rained in a very long time, and the enormity of the task was incomprehensible. It is recorded the Ark was equal to one and a half football fields in length, and as tall as a four-story building. God gave Noah very strict directions on what kind of wood to use, how high, long and wide it had to be, where to put the doors, and how many decks it needed. Scholars have estimated that the Ark held almost 45,000 animals. Now that is one big boat!

When God called upon him, Noah had two choices: to obey and trust God, or tell God "No, I'm just not ready to take on such a 'God-sized' project." How many times in our lives have we said "NO" to God when he has asked us to step out in faith and obedience to do something for him? What would have happened if Noah did not obey and trust God? God knew that Noah was a man after his heart. He knew Noah was faithful and that he and his family worshiped Him, so He went to the one man on all the earth that would listen and obey. After God had spoken to Noah, Noah got right to work building the Ark, and twice in the Bible it says, "Noah did everything just as God commanded him." Noah listened to every detail the Lord had told him as to how to build the Ark, what kind and how many animals to bring on board, and anything else that God told him to do.

And God will do the same with us. He will guide us through any project or vision with the same details and wisdom that only comes from God through the working of the Holy Spirit in us. We are powerless, but God is powerful. He is the vine, and we are the branches; we must stay connected to him to receive his power. He will give us what we need to accomplish any task for Him. And most of the time, God will call us to do that one thing we have no talent for, or have the natural ability to pull off. That is because God says, "… my power is made perfect in weakness" 2 Corinthians 12:9. If He always used us in our areas of strength, we wouldn't need to rely on Him, and He wouldn't get all the glory! God wants other people to see Him working through us and using His power to get things done.

We also should note that Noah wasn't a perfect person. He had his moments just as we all do. He grew a vineyard, got drunk on the wine made from the grapes, and ended up lying naked under his tent. His sons, embarrassed for him, covered him up. This isn't something you would expect from a man of God, but God knew that Noah wasn't "perfect." He knew that Noah worshipped him and loved him with all his heart, mind, and soul, which is why God could use him. God also knows we are imperfect human beings in an imperfect world, and He still loves us and wants to use us for his purposes. No one is too much of a "sinner" to be used by God. He can use anyone who is devoted to him, is obedient, and trusts Him for the outcome.

## POINTS TO PONDER

Trusting in God is something the people in the Bible did long ago. We need to rely on God for protection, for guidance, and for daily living. Have you trusted God in the following areas of your life?

- Protection from a potential hazard? What could have happened if God did not intervene?

- Taking on something you're not particularly gifted at? How did it turn out? Did you see God's hand in it?

- Doing something that seems crazy at the time? Did you pray and still seem led by God to try it?

- Being obedient and following through on a project? How did being obedient feel? Did it bless others?

Pray today for the Holy Spirit to strengthen your trust in God and help you to rely on Him for everything.

*Therefore I tell you, whatever you ask for*
*in prayer, believe that you have received it,*
*and it will be yours.*

Mark 11:24

CHAPTER EIGHT

# Noel the Kitten, Moving Again, and the Letter

It was Christmastime and things were bustling. Everyone was busy shopping for gifts, attending parties, and happily preparing for the festivities of the season. We were no different, and life was kind of crazy. Two weeks before Christmas, my daughter called to tell me she had been given a nine-week-old black and white kitten by her soon to be mother-in-law. The kitten was appropriately named "Noel." I was thrilled for her. I had two cats of my own and loved them deeply. When she told me the kitten was very sick, I was devastated. I asked her what I could do to help. The kitten needed to go the vet, but my daughter had come down with the flu. She asked if I could take Noel to the vet. I agreed and left quickly.

When I saw Noel, all I wanted to do was cuddle her in my arms. I carefully placed Noel in the pet carrier and headed to the vet. They concluded that she had an infection in her lungs and prescribed antibiotics. Because she was so young and very ill, they gave me special food to feed her, too. They instructed me to feed her by putting the food on my finger. I was handed a dropper with which to give her as much water as possible. They didn't know if she would make it or not.

I called my daughter after I left the vet's office and explained the situation to her. She worked full-time and was afraid she wouldn't be able to give Noel the proper care but she would try. After a couple of days, Noel worsened. Well-meaning friends tried to convince my daughter that it might be better to "put Noel down" instead of spending the time and money on such a sick kitty. She called me to discuss this. My heart sank, and the Lord spoke to me that this kitty was not to be "put down" but to be cared for and nurtured. I asked if I could take her home with me. I said this without even considering the fact that I had two cats at home that would have to be quarantined from Noel, nor without asking my husband if it was OK. My daughter agreed to let me take her.

I settled Noel in our bedroom and closed the doors. This room would be her new home so she could recover away from the other cats, but in a small enough area that I could keep a close eye on her. I knew John would not be thrilled having a cat, even a small sick cat in the bedroom because he is allergic to cats. However, being the gracious husband he is, he agreed it was OK for now.

Over the next few days, I sat in the bathroom and fed her very small amounts of moist food from my fingertip and coaxed her to drink water from the dropper. I stroked her and prayed over her every day asking God to heal this poor little kitten. She was too weak to play, choosing to lie in her bed and sleep. She was holding her own. By now, Christmas was over, and we were headed toward New Year's. On the morning of New Year's Eve, I noticed she was having a hard time breathing. She was gasping for air and looked to be in distress. I called the vet who encouraged me to bring her in right away. They drew blood and put her in an oxygen chamber in an attempt to get more air into her lungs. The vet told me I had to leave her there for a few days. I cuddled Noel gently, prayed over her, and left with tears in my eyes. I asked God to watch over her.

The following day, I received a phone call from the vet. She told me Noel had almost died three times the night before but was revived each time. The results of the blood test showed her white blood cell count was at 70,000. A normal white cell count was 11,000. The vet said I could pick her up the following morning, but not to expect too much and to prepare myself that she wouldn't make it. Noel was put on a new antibiotic, but the vet wasn't sure if it would do any good. I hung up the phone and thanked God for keeping Noel alive so far. I told him I believed He was going to heal her.

I brought Noel home the next morning. This was it—either God would heal her or He would call her home. Over the next seven days, I continued to feed her, give her water, and administer the antibiotics. She had her blood drawn again, and the white blood cell count was still elevated above 70,000 so it didn't look like the antibiotics were working. The vet said there was nothing else they could do; she told me to prepare myself for Noel not to make it. Something inside of me refused to give up on this kitten. She had already fought to stay alive this long, and I knew God heard my prayers. I then did something radical. I threw the last two doses of her antibiotics into the trashcan and told the good Lord that Noel was completely in His hands. I would just wait on Him and trust Him. I went to bed that night and felt a peace come over me about Noel. Two days later, I walked into the bedroom to get something. Noel wasn't lying in her bed. I looked around the bedroom for her afraid of what I might find. Suddenly, she darted out from under our bed. She was running around playing with something. I was stunned. I watched her run around the room like a normal healthy kitten should. My eyes filled with tears once again. I knew that God had healed her. She began eating and drinking on her own soon after that. When I released her to the rest of the house to meet her two cat brothers, she instantly started fighting with and bullying them! They couldn't believe this tiny little kitten was so mighty and unafraid. She hasn't had any health problems since; she was completely healed by God. Noel became a permanent member of our household, to our great joy. She has the ability to charm anyone, even if they aren't cat lovers. Visitors to our home can't get enough of her sweetness, tenderness, and playful spirit. I thanked God that he used me and didn't let Noel be put down. God gets all the glory for saving this cat.

## MOVING AGAIN

We never regretted buying the home we purchased before our wedding. The large backyard allowed us to host two very special events: my parents' fiftieth wedding anniversary party and a wedding reception for my son and his bride.

But after living in the house for two years, it was starting to feel like a money pit. We groaned when we thought about how much money we had spent on fixing the house up before we moved in. At the time, we justified it as necessary to make the house "work for us." Then there was the money needed for the upkeep of the yard, the monthly house payment, and numerous other bills. It felt like a very heavy burden. One day, as I wrote out the check for the house payment, the burden became too much. I thought, "How ridiculous it is to be spending so much money on ourselves just to have this beautiful house."

We wanted to be following the Lord, which meant getting our finances in order and being a blessing to others. That's tough to do when you are in debt up to your eyeballs. While I sat in contemplation, the Lord spoke to my heart. He told me it was time to get things right in our lives, to stop living for ourselves and all the luxuries this world has to offer, get out of debt, and live in the freedom of being able to give to others who are in need.

I have to admit, I was OK with this. I came from a humble upbringing and most of my life I lived in small homes and enjoyed a modest budget. I knew I could go back to that, and I would much rather live that way then be stressed out financially and not following God's path. The next step was to approach my husband with this revelation. I prayed about it, and then spoke with John about what I felt the Lord was saying to me. At first, he was a bit reluctant. His points, while valid, didn't sway me. He pointed out that we had lived in this house such a short time; we had moved twice before we were married two years ago, and it was our dream house with the perfect backyard. But after we discussed our mound of debt, our commitment to God, and our desire to give more to others, we decided together that putting the house up for sale was the right thing to do.

*If anyone has material possessions and sees his*
*brother in need but has no pity on him, how can*
*the love of God be in him?*
1 John 3:17

We called a real estate agent we knew and started the process of selling and moving again. Our timing wasn't great; the real estate market was just beginning to tank. It took six months to sell our house, just in the nick of time for us, but perfect timing by God's clock.

Since we were downsizing, we put some of our household items, such as antiques, up for sale also. This helped the amount of "stuff" we had to move, and helped pay off some of the debt. We sold off all possessions that didn't have any meaning or significance. We rummaged through everything. We were committed to getting out of debt and starting fresh.

While waiting for the house to sell, we stumbled upon a small piece of land out in the country, which we both fell in love with. So we bought it with the intention of building a small home on it. We met with architects who drew up the plans. We had to wait on the sale of the house in order to have the cash in hand to pay for its construction. In the interim, we had to rent a house until the new one was finished. We found a rental near the new home site that was a perfect fit. It was small, but the price was right. Once the house sold, we again had to go through the whole moving process of packing everything, taking only what we needed, and storing anything we could live without for the next year. I thought it was funny that we could store something for a whole year, never really miss or need it, and yet think that after a year we're going to need it again.

John and I had the best times in that small, simple home. When we sold the big house, we were able to pay off all of our debt, and so we really were living a simple lifestyle. What a joy it was.

As we continued with the plans for the new home, I kept thinking how far away from everything we were going to be, even though it was lovely countryside. I was also concerned with how the expenses for this "new small home" kept going up. I was becoming a little discouraged about it all, so one day while John and I were out on a walk, I asked him his thoughts on these two subjects. It was as if God had already prepared his heart for this talk. He told me he really didn't want to live so far out and that the cost of the new house was becoming way too much. He agreed with everything that was on my heart, so we decided that God was leading us on a different path. We were not to build a new home, but find something small closer in to where we had lived before. I know this sounds a little crazy with all the moving, changing of decisions, and back and forth, but going on an adventure with God is usually like this. Sometimes God has to beat us over the head numerous times until we are in His will, following His path, and determining to obey Him. He wants to show us the best way, yet it's so easy to get wrapped up in the world and what we think we want. It is much harder to ask God what He wants for us, and then take the initiative to follow. This is what John and I wanted for our lives now, to follow God's plan, not ours.

When we started looking for a cottage to buy, it didn't take long to find the perfect place in a neighborhood we loved. We paid cash for the nearly ninety-year-old house and had some left to do some much-needed updating. God blessed us with a cozy, comfortable cottage we love. I thank you, Lord, for leading us, guiding us, and speaking to us in the midst of our sinful lives. God really does care about everything in our lives and He and only He knows what is best for us.

## THE LETTER

During the year in our rental home, we traveled to Florida to see my son, his wife, and our first granddaughter. She was just a few months old, and I couldn't wait to see her and visit with them. We had a great time, but my heart was heavy as we returned home. Despite the outward appearance of an OK relationship with my son, many hurtful things had happened during his childhood that put a wedge between us.

I got pregnant with my son at nineteen, married his father, and moved far away from my family and friends. I was unprepared for my new life. I did the best I could but I divorced his father when he was just four years old. I decided to take my nine-month-old daughter, his sister, and move back to St. Louis. I left my son with his dad in California. At the time, I believed this to be the best thing—for me, at least. There were other factors that played into this decision, but ultimately I was the one who left.

Today, it's unimaginable how I could have done this. I didn't know the Lord at the time, so it was all about my so-called "happiness" and me. I wasn't thinking about anyone other than myself and what I wanted to get out of my life. I wasn't concerned about hurting someone I loved dearly to get what I wanted, or thought I wanted. It was in the depths of selfishness that I said good-bye to my sweet boy.

Not surprisingly, I struggled through life for a couple of years, always feeling like a part of me was missing. I had such guilty feelings about my son and filled my life with whatever I could to numb the pain. I kept in contact with him, and when he and his dad moved back to St. Louis, I was able to start seeing him every other weekend.

I eventually remarried. As he got older, he spent more time with us, even going on vacations. Thankfully, we had a relationship, but there was still a hole in my heart about what I had done earlier in his life. It wasn't just a guilty feeling in me. My son demonstrated how he felt through his actions—conscious or not.

Once, they spent a week in St. Louis. We saw them for only three hours. I called late in their visit only to learn they were already on the road headed back to Florida, with no good-bye. I was devastated. I knew things weren't right. I cried, got mad, and had no idea what to do about it. It was then the Lord spoke to me and revealed the fact that I had never really asked my son to forgive me for leaving him as a little boy. This sweet little boy, who didn't deserve to be treated so poorly, had a deep hurt inside because his mother walked out on him. It was like a large knife stabbed its way through my heart. I was utterly crushed. It was true. I had never asked his forgiveness for what I had done. The ugliness of my oversight hit me hard. I didn't think I would ever stop crying.

> *I speak the truth in Christ—I am not lying, my*
> *conscience confirms it in the Holy Spirit—I have*
> *great sorrow and unceasing anguish in my heart.*
> Romans 9:1-2

In the midst of my sorrow, our Heavenly Father spoke ever so softly to me and told me to write him a letter to apologize for hurting him. The next day, I began a soul-searching journey to understand my actions so long ago. I poured out my heart out to him about my sorrow, selfishness, pride, and poor choices. I wrote I wished I could go back and make it all better and be the mom he had needed me to be. I wrote of my mistakes I had made along the way, and asked him to forgive the past me, and love me for who I am now. I expressed how much I loved him and wanted a relationship with him, his wife, and daughter. I told him how much I cherished any time I could spend with him, how proud I was of him and what he had accomplished in life, and what an awesome father he was. I ended by telling him I was praying for God to help him forgive me, something I so longed for. I had to stop writing several times, because the pain was just too much. It was devastating to think of what I had done and how it affected everyone around me.

It took me a couple of days to finish the letter. I sealed the letter in the envelope and put it in my dresser drawer. I needed some time to pray and ponder about what I had written and what the outcome might be if I sent it. Would he accept it? Would he even read it? What if somehow it made things worse? My concerns felt real; I also knew God would speak to me about it.

The next night, I was awakened from a deep sleep. I sat straight up in bed, feeling as if God had just said aloud, "Mail that letter tomorrow. What are you waiting for? Trust me." I laid there wide-awake with tears in my eyes as I thanked God for speaking to me so clearly. The next morning, I dropped my letter into the mailbox along with a prayer to the Lord. The outcome was up to my son and God. I couldn't go back and change things, as much as I wanted to. All I could do was hope for a brighter future with my son.

I mailed my letter a few days before Mother's Day. I hadn't planned that, so when my son called me on Mother's Day, I knew that he must have received my letter. The healing process was beginning. We have never talked about the letter, but I do thank the Lord every day for guiding me, helping me to recognize my sins, humble myself, and ask for forgiveness from Him and from my son.

We all make mistakes in life; the question is whether we're willing to take a long hard look at ourselves and change what needs to be changed, regardless of the outcome. Will we trust God to help us make those changes that will affect others and us for a lifetime? I pray that we will ask the Lord to reveal any sins that have not been dealt with, and that we will lean on the Lord and the Holy Spirit to work in us and through us to help accomplish these things.

## POINTS TO PONDER

Sometimes in life we just need to cry and pray and let God mold our hearts and help us work on changing our thinking. We can then work on readjusting our perspective and changing what might need to be changed. Ask God to help you in the following ways:

- To give you a trusting heart for sicknesses to be healed. In what ways do you need to increase your faith in this area?

- To help you seek forgiveness for yourself and from others and admit your mistakes. Who are the people in your life you have been able to forgive, and what do you still need to forgive yourself for?

- To move you closer to his plan for your life. What do you think your purpose is here on earth, and are you willing to obey it?

- To give you hope of a brighter future and leave the past behind. What does living one day at a time feel like to you? What in your past still needs to be dealt with?

Every day is a new beginning, and we can move closer to the heart of God as we grow and learn.

*Call to me and I will answer you and tell you great*
*and unsearchable things you do not know.*

Jeremiah 33:3

CHAPTER NINE

# Burkina Faso
# and the Orphanage

In the first chapter, I wrote about how God showed me that I was to go to Uganda with John. In early November, a couple of months before we were to leave for Uganda, John decided to do a little research on a product called "Plumpynut." Plumpynut is a peanut-butter-based protein supplement that helps malnourished children in third-world countries. During his research, he came across a man in St. Louis who was familiar with the product, so he emailed him and asked if they could get together to discuss this product and the current market for it in Africa. The man responded by email that he would be happy to, but currently he was in Burkina Faso, Africa, and wouldn't be home for a while. Neither of us had heard of "Burkina Faso," so we looked it up on the internet. It was in a region of Africa that used to be called "Upper Volta." It's considered one of the three poorest countries in the world, largely because it sits in the very hot, dry desert.

A few days later, we visited a store that sold "fair trade" items from around the world. We were surprised at the variety of items for sale from different parts of the world. My husband, being the inquisitive one, approached the owner and asked her some questions. She told us that she had spent about three months studying textiles in a small country in Africa named "Burkina Faso." Imagine our surprise at hearing twice about a place in Africa named Burkina Faso that we had never heard of before. We were beginning to think something was going on.

The next day was Saturday and John decided to help at an inner city church where a workshop on fixing bikes for kids was being held. He hadn't done this before, so when he arrived, he sought out the man in charge. As they talked, he told John that he and his wife felt called to be missionaries and that they really wanted to go to Burkina Faso. John couldn't believe it—three mentions in three days. Now we were convinced something important was happening, but we didn't know what. We decided to pray to God about what He was doing and ask Him to reveal it to us.

The December rush was on, and we were at a Christmas party. About halfway through the evening, I struck up a conversation with a friend by saying, "Hey, did you hear that I am going to Africa on a mission trip?" She replied, "You aren't going to Burkina Faso, are you?" I'm sure my mouth dropped open. I asked her why in the world she would ask me that. She told me that in the past week, she had heard about Burkina Faso three times, and was going to a Bible study class at a church that sent people on a mission trip there every other year. I told her she needed to talk with John about this, because we had heard Burkina Faso three times as well. These revelations freaked us both out a bit because she had never heard of it before either. We now all wondered what God was up to. My friend said she would try to find out some additional information about it through her Bible study. She called me a couple of days later to say there was an orphanage in Burkina Faso, run by a woman named Ruth Cox. That was all she knew. I thanked her for the information and relayed it to John. Burkina Faso would have to wait, as we prepared for our journey to Uganda. Burkina Faso, however, did not want to wait.

Exhausted and on the final leg of our trip home from Uganda, John and I looked for a way to spend the time. We both picked up the movie schedule for the flight. I think we both said, "Oh!" when we spotted the listing for a documentary about wrestlers in Burkina Faso. This was becoming commonplace; we looked at each other and laughed.

There was a woman sitting next to John, and he struck up a conversation with her. She told him a few things and then, unexpectedly, said, "My father is actually a pastor and he served in a small country in Africa for about three months, in Burkina Faso. Only an all-powerful God, who desperately wants to speak with us, and show us His will, can make these kinds of events happen in our lives. That plane probably had over four hundred people on board, and we just "happened" to be seated next to a woman whose father served in Burkina Faso. There are no coincidences.

God orchestrates everything in our lives. If we are listening every day, we will be witness to the amazing things that happen beyond our control. That is, of course, because God has control over everything in our lives. He also has a purpose for each of us. If our eyes and ears are open and available, He will clearly show us. What a comfort it is to know also that He has the big plan already prepared for us. We just have to follow Him, diligently.

In late February, John volunteered at a legal clinic in the inner city. On this day, a couple needed some legal advice because the man was hit by a car as he rode his bike. During their talk, the wife shared how they wanted to be missionaries and had applied to the mission board. This sparked John's interest, and he asked them where they wanted to go. She replied, "Burkina Faso; I grew up there." Once again, another "Burkina Faso Sighting" as we now called them. Seven times now we've heard about this country without knowing what God's will is for this place half way around the world.

Over the next month, we had a few more amazing things happen; and so did my friend, Brenna. One Thursday night, she woke up, sat straight up in bed, and felt compelled to get on Facebook. She did, even though it was after midnight. To her amazement, Ruth Cox, the missionary working at Sheltering Wings Orphanage in Burkina Faso, was online. We later learned Ruth only got online about twice a month, and usually for only about 20 minutes. When Brenna saw Ruth online, she immediately started a conversation with her. Ruth told her that she was coming back to the States in March and staying through April to do some fundraising and get a little rest. Brenna called us excitedly the next day to tell us the news. We all hoped we would get to meet Ruth while she was visiting.

Brenna tried repeatedly to get in touch with Ruth Cox. She tried emailing and calling, but she couldn't reach her. I shared this news with John one morning. We had still been praying for the Lord to show us what His will was for Burkina Faso. John called me mid-morning that same day, and said, "Guess who I just spoke with?" I asked, and he said, "Ruth Cox." I asked him how and he said, "I just looked up the phone number for Sheltering Wings on the Internet and called it, and she answered." God definitely wanted us to meet her. She was in St. Louis and was to call me later to set up a meeting with her. The puzzle pieces were starting to fit together, but we had no idea how well until much later.

Our meeting with Ruth was set for Sunday, March 29, in the late afternoon. Three couples wanted to meet her and discuss her needs at the orphanage. The meeting was set, and we were going to get to meet Ruth Cox, who lived half way around the world in a small country named Burkina Faso in Africa. Isn't God truly awesome that He could orchestrate the chain of events that would lead us to this day! I still just sit in awe of a God who is so real in our everyday lives and who can guide our steps if we listen. Remember, the key here is listening and being aware when God is speaking to us. Nothing is coincidental. Everything that happens, everything that is said, everyone we meet, is orchestrated by God to fulfill His purpose for our lives. We only have choices to make—do we listen and pay attention, or do we shrug it off and say it doesn't mean anything.

A week before our meeting with Ruth Cox, John took a woman's van to be worked on by a fellow church member who has a ministry of fixing vehicles for the less fortunate. As they talked, this man mentioned his daughter had wanted to be a missionary for the last seven years. At the age of fourteen, she found an article entitled *The Gospel according to Ruth*, and it sparked her interest. It was an article about Ruth and the orphanage she had started the year before. This young girl vowed to be a missionary in Burkina Faso someday. Seven years later, she met Ruth Cox. Again, God works in people's lives orchestrating events for years later.

Another thing happened a week before our meeting with Ruth. We had been talking about replacing the deck and the wooden fence in our backyard. So, we had the fence guy over to give us a bid. A friend who owns a remodeling business also came over to draw up a plan to replace the old deck with one twice as big with an attached screened-in room and ceiling fan. We decided to use cedar to build the deck and fence.

I felt uneasy about spending all this money, but I put it out of my mind. The next day, I woke up feeling "off." Something wasn't right with me, so as John was getting ready to head out to the store, I told him I would just stay home and read a little. I usually first read in my Bible, but this morning I didn't feel lead to read anywhere in particular. Instead, I picked up a book called *The Hole in Our Gospel*, written by Richard Stearns, the president of World Vision. His book had been released four weeks earlier, and I was really moved while reading it. I had read two chapters when a scripture jumped off the page at me. I decided to look up that scripture in my Bible.

It was Jeremiah 22:16. Whenever I look up a scripture, I always read some above and some below so I can understand the full meaning. I began reading at Jeremiah 22:14, "He says, 'I will build myself a great palace with spacious upper rooms.' So he makes large windows in it, panels it with cedar and decorates it in red." I stop and look around. The room I am in is paneled in cedar and painted red. Chills ran through my body at this realization. I sat still pondering what I had just read. How could it describe where I was sitting? How would God know that one scripture would jump out at me? Of all the words in the Bible, how did I stumble upon these words? Once again, God orchestrates everything for His good and the good of His Kingdom.

I continued reading, Jeremiah 22:15 said, "Does it make you a king to have more and more cedar?" Is God asking me if it makes me a king (or a queen) to have more and more cedar? We're going to build the deck and fence out of cedar. Does that make me feel more important or more successful? I stopped to consider what I had read. I never in a million years thought that I would see the word cedar in the Bible, and certainly not be drawn to that scripture the day after our friend was at the house talking about our cedar deck and cedar fence.

I read on…Jeremiah 22:16, "He defended the cause of the poor and needy, and so all went well. Is that not what it means to know me, declares the Lord." It was clear to me. God was speaking, very clearly, saying, "Do not spend that money on yourselves for that cedar deck and fence. You are to use it for the causes of the poor and needy." I sat there; I couldn't move. I was in awe of what I had just witnessed God saying to me.

I know many minutes passed before I heard John drive up. As soon as he walked in the door, he told me how upset he was that the store he went to would not sell him the cedar play set he wanted to buy for our grandchild. I just laughed. I asked him to sit down so I could read something to him and asked that he share his thoughts after I was finished reading. He agreed.

I read the entire scripture, watching John's face. I saw his eyes get bigger and bigger. By the time I finished, even his mouth was hanging open in shock. Then he spoke. "We should not build the deck or put the fence in, but need to use that money for the poor and needy." There was the confirmation I needed; he felt the same way I did. Then we both just sat there in amazement about how God was able to stop us dead in our tracks from doing the wrong thing with the money that God had entrusted to us to use in His Kingdom. I felt like the message was loud and clear, kind of like when my mother was standing over me shaking her finger and telling me that I had better not do something, or else! When that happened, I knew I had better obey my mother,or there would be some serious consequences to face later on. I know that we serve a loving God, but I also know that making the wrong choices in our lives will most of the time be connected with facing the consequences of that wrong choice. I, personally, through many trials and wrong choices over the years, would rather obey than face the consequences. It is obedience mixed in with a little fear, which I think is OK.

It didn't escape us that we would be meeting with Ruth Cox for the first time to discuss her needs at the orphanage. This was another example of God's excellent timing. It couldn't have been more perfect!

On Sunday, we met with Ruth Cox. She is a wonderful, compassionate, soft-spoken woman with a warm, loving smile. She spoke with love about the children at her orphanage and discussed with us the needs and concerns they face in Burkina Faso. She showed us pictures of the children, the orphanage, and the school. As she shared her stories with us, my heart was breaking for these children. It wasn't fair. Why do they have so little, and we and our children are so blessed? Why do we have beds to sleep in, kitchens to cook in, and a closet full of clothes to wear? They don't even have a kitchen at the orphanage, just an outdoor pit. Clothes and especially beds are luxuries. I believe that God never planned for there to be such a large division between the poor and the rich. I believe that God planned on all of us using what He has given us, in abundance, and sharing that with the less fortunate. Why aren't we doing this?

*Now all who believed were together,*

*and had all things in common, and sold their*

*possessions and goods, and divided them among*

*all, as anyone had need.*

Acts 2:44-45

We are supposed to have concern for each other's material needs so that all are provided for. It also says in Proverbs 3:27-28, "Do not withhold good from those to whom it is due, when it is in the power of your hand to do so. Do not say to your neighbor, 'Come back later; I will give it tomorrow,' when you now have it with you." Everyone in the world is our neighbor and God cares for us, so let us care for others.

I asked Ruth what the most pressing issue was at the orphanage currently. She replied that they really needed to build three more rooms to adequately accommodate the 145 children attending the school. I asked her if she had an estimate on what that might cost to build. She did and told us the amount. To my and John's utter shock and amazement, it was the exact amount of money we would have spent on the deck and fence for our house. I paused for a moment unable to speak, again in awe of a God who has this kind of power. He knew the needs of His children in Burkina Faso. He, through His Word, opened our eyes to their needs, and lovingly encouraged us to spend, what He had given us, not on ourselves, but on the less fortunate children at this orphanage. Could there be anything more wonderful and fulfilling than seeing God's plan for our lives come to fruition?

We didn't say anything to Ruth at that moment and arranged to meet with her again the following Tuesday morning. Monday evening, John said he felt like we were supposed to do a "matching gift challenge" and hold a fundraiser to raise even more money for the orphanage. I told him that if he felt like God was leading us to do that, it was fine with me. When we met with Ruth, we told her our deck and fence story, and how we felt God wanted us to give that money to the orphanage. We also shared the idea of a matching gift challenge. She started crying. Ruth told us that a man on Sheltering Wings board said that when he was praying, he felt someone was going to give a large sum of money and that it would be for a "matching gift challenge." The three of us sat there, tears welling up in our eyes. This all seemed so impossible, yet, God's power is larger and more alive than we ever thought possible.

The "Dessert Night" Fundraiser we designed was delicious and a huge success. Ruth captivated the audience as she described the situation and surroundings in Burkina. Her slideshow brought tears to the eyes of many. Donations came in, questions were answered, and a few children were sponsored. At the end of the night, we felt confident that God was there in the midst of it all, and within the next week, after all the lingering contributors had announced their giving, a grand total of $88,000 had been raised for Sheltering Wings.

The only way to describe this feat was that God's power and glory were shown at this specific time to bless this organization that was helping orphans and widows. John and I were blessed to be a part of this event and to witness the unbelievable generosity of the people God had assigned to be a part of it. Did we miss not having a new deck or fence? Not in the least, because we experienced what it was like to be obedient to the Lord and be blessed in so many ways.

We realized that material objects are so much less attractive than striving for the rewards we will receive in heaven for being obedient here on earth. Every time we sat on that old, ugly deck, we would smile and thank God for the lesson we had learned. I can only hope that this inspires you to actively search for God every day and listen to that still, small voice inside of you telling you which way to turn, right or left, to follow our Heavenly Father. It will undoubtedly be the ride of your life if you choose to get on and take a chance. Don't hesitate, you won't be disappointed.

## POINTS TO PONDER

God can orchestrate anything. How often do you think about a need halfway around the world and imagine that God could use you to satisfy that need? Almost sounds impossible, doesn't it? And yet we know that "all things are possible with God." So what can you do?

- Listen to the "still, small voice" in your head. How have you responded when you felt God speaking to you about something?

- Pay attention to what is going on around you. When have you seen God orchestrating something right in front of you?

- Keep praying about what God's will is. How often do you have a "quiet time" with God in prayer?

- Never "doubt" when God speaks to you. Has God asked you to do something, but you have hesitated to act on it?

His plans and ways are always bigger than ours are, so challenge your small dreams to make way for God-sized dreams.

*The Lord will guide you always; he will satisfy your*
*needs in a sun-scorched land and will strengthen*
*your frame. You will be a well-watered garden, like*
*a spring whose waters never fail.*
Isaiah 58:11

CHAPTER TEN

# My Second Trip to Africa, The Head Cold, and the "700 Club"

God's work was changing lives at Sheltering Wings. Nine months after the dessert fundraiser, John wanted to see first-hand what changes were taking place and understand the organization more fully. A trip to Burkina Faso with another couple and a videographer was planned for the following January.

Our travel was uneventful. We arrived on schedule, and Ruth picked us up from the airport. It was great to see her again. We drove for two hours from Ouagadougou, the capital of Burkina Faso, to get to Yako, where the orphanage and school are located. When we arrived, we unpacked and were given our room assignments. The accommodations were nice, but not like homes in the States. There wasn't any air conditioning and no hot water for showering. In addition, only a tin roof separated us from two-foot long lizards that, if they wanted to, could climb to get into the bedrooms! Luckily, John and I never had a problem, but Scott, rooming next to us, did. He had a lizard climb in and curl up on his bed. He promptly left his room, closed the door, and slept on the couch in the open area of the home. The next morning, the guys had to capture the lizard in a plastic bin and take him outside! Fortunately, there were no more problems with the lizards, but Scott slept with one eye open at night!

The next couple of days were spent meeting teachers at the school, some of the workers and the children at the orphanage, and going to other villages nearby. The highlight of the trip for me was meeting our three sponsored children.

On the day we were to meet Nomwendi and her mother, I was very emotional. I was excited about meeting her, and I was very nervous, too. I began crying as we were driving out to her village. God was preparing my heart for this extraordinary meeting with this young girl and her mother. Scott video recorded this precious moment for us, and I never imagined how wonderful it would be or how much I would treasure it.

As Nomwendi walked toward us holding her mother's hand, I couldn't contain myself. I began walking toward her, too. With an interpreter's help, I introduced myself to them. Then I gave them both a big hug. John stood nearby quietly at first. He didn't want to scare them since it was unlikely they had seen "white folks" before. We talked for a couple of minutes and gave them a few gifts such as, material to make a new dress, school paper and pens.

We held hands and walked through the village to their home. When we arrived, they invited us in. Their small mud hut was only ten feet by eight feet and had a dirt floor. There were a couple of mats on the ground, which they slept on at night, and a few pots they used for cooking over an open fire outside the hut. They had one chair and really, that was it. I was quite humbled by their meager circumstances. I thanked God we were able to help this girl and her mother who lived with so few necessities. We talked with them a few minutes more and then it was time to go.

We took pictures and thanked them for showing us their home. They walked with us out into the courtyard. John and I gave both of them another hug. I started sobbing uncontrollably as we walked toward our vehicle. I was in awe that John and I had just met our sponsored child who lived halfway around the world. She wasn't just a picture on a paper but a human being who needed help to go to school and have a lunch to eat every day. She and her mother were so sweet, humble, and appreciative of what we were doing for them, yet for us it was such a small sacrifice to make to help someone in need. To see the village where they lived and their mud hut was a sobering event. We live with so much in the United States that we can grow insensitive to how other people are just trying to survive. I was so thankful to have met Nomwendi and her mother. This meeting was, for me, the chance of a lifetime, and one I will never forget.

Over the next few days, we also met our two sponsored boys, which was an equally wonderful experience. The boys were doing well in school and seemed happy and healthy considering their living conditions. It is still amazing to me how happy the people in Africa are when you consider how little they have, and the harsh conditions they live in. We could all learn some valuable lessons from them, and I know that I will never be the same because of my journeys to Africa.

## THE HEAD COLD

February in St. Louis is often not only cold, frosty, and gloomy but also the month when viruses and flu bugs run rampant. Because of the dire warnings for a bad flu season, I had gotten a flu shot, which I typically don't do, at the end of November. True to the predictions, it was an extremely bad flu season. I escaped the ravaging bug through December and January, and thought that I just might be in the clear because I had gotten "the shot." Well, to my dismay, I started feeling as if a head cold was coming on in early February. I thought it wouldn't be too bad, just a head cold. When I awoke the next morning, I knew that my small, simple head cold was turning into a head-pounding, nasal congested, crappy feeling full-blown virus. "The shot" had failed me. At John's suggestion, I started taking some medicine every few hours to relieve my symptoms. It did seem to help. But I wasn't getting any better, so I called my homeopathic doctor to see what he might recommend. During my appointment, he told me about an all-natural injection they could give me that would "dry me up" within twenty-four hours. Well, Hallelujah! I thanked the Lord that He was going to take care of me.

The nurse gave me the injection in my neck. Almost immediately, I knew something didn't feel right. I had the feeling I had done something wrong, but I couldn't get out of it or take it back. Unfortunately, I was right. That evening, I noticed my mouth was starting to feel extremely dry, way more than usual, so I started sipping on more water. By bedtime, my mouth had become so dry that I had to sip water every minute or two. I was unable to sleep all night because I couldn't swallow without some extra water in my mouth. I had never experienced anything like this before in my life. I was so miserable, and the extreme dryness was starting to scare me. The next day wasn't any better. I lay on the couch all day sipping water, barely able to swallow without that extra moisture.

That night, no sleep again. For three nights, I sat straight up on the couch trying to sleep a few minutes at a time. The lack of sleep started to take its toll on me. By Saturday that week, I was in bed the whole day exhausted from no sleep. The virus wouldn't leave me. At this point, I was depressed, upset, angry, and wondering why this was happening to me. Interestingly enough, I hadn't been praying much during this illness. I was so wrapped up in trying to help myself get through it that I had forgotten to call on God for help.

Just before 1:00 a.m. Monday morning, I was sitting on the couch with my head in my hands, asking God to speak to me, show me what was going on, what I needed to see, and help me understand it. I prayed for a few minutes, and then a thought popped into

GOD SPEAKS...ARE YOU LISTENING?

my head. I needed to go into the bathroom, turn on the hot water, close the door, and create a "steam room" effect to help my nose and head open up so I could breathe better. I didn't have anything else to do, or a better idea, so I did as I was instructed. I decided to read my Bible

It fell open to Isaiah 1, and I started reading there. Verse 5 got my attention when I read the words, "Your whole head is injured." I knew I needed to keep reading. I continued on to Isaiah 2, and noticed I had something highlighted from before, Isaiah 2:11, "The eyes of the arrogant man will be humbled and the pride of men brought low; the Lord alone will be exalted in that day." As I read on to Isaiah 2:22, "Stop trusting in man, who has but a breath in his nostrils. Of what account is he?" Wasn't I sitting in my bathroom at 1:00 a.m., trying desperately to get some steam into my "injured head" so I could "breathe through my nostrils?" There was no doubt in my mind. God was speaking to me. He showed me that He knew exactly what was happening to me at that moment, and He was speaking about my trust in man, and not in Him! I was humbled; I had been asking everyone else's opinion on what to do, instead of going to the one who knows everything and trusting Him!

The Bible explains it in these terms—people are very limited when compared to God, they can be unreliable and shortsighted. Yet, we trust our lives and futures more to human beings than to the all-knowing God. Only God is completely reliable. Psalm 139:13-16 tells us that He created us and knit us together in our mother's womb. He knows us better than anyone does, and He ordained all our days before one of them came to be. Psalm 105:4 says "Look to the Lord and his strength; seek his face always."

Yes, God was speaking loud and clear to me. Why had I not gone to Him in prayer and just asked Him to give me the strength to get through this trial? Why had I relied on other people's opinions, which got me into more trouble, instead of asking the One who knows what is best for me in any situation? The answer was simply because I am human, and I am a sinner. I am far from perfect, and I will make mistakes in this life here on earth. At times, I will want to trust in my own strength, or wisdom, or resources rather than turning to the all-knowing and powerful God for my answers. Oh, the lessons we must learn!

I finally left the bathroom but couldn't pull myself away from the Bible. I sat up reading until around 4:00 a.m. and then went to bed and slept for almost four hours. When I woke up, I thanked God for that long sleep, the first in almost a week. Since I was awake, I opened my Bible again. That day my recovery started, spiritually and physically. God continued to speak to me through His words. Psalm 31:14-15, "But I trust in you, O Lord; I say, 'You are my God.' My times are in your hands; deliver me from my enemies and from those who pursue me." By saying this, we are expressing our belief that all of life's circumstances are under God's control. We know that God loves and cares for us enables us to keep steady in our faith regardless of our circumstances. It keeps us from sinning foolishly by taking matters into our own hands or resenting God's timetable.

I continued my recovery for the next five days. I slept a lot and spent a lot of time in God's word. I learned many lessons through this time of trial and sickness, and I am thankful that God cares enough about me to show me the things in my life I need to work on and change. Unless we are able to see and hear these things, and then try to apply them in our lives, we will always be striving for things in this world that are meaningless and unreliable. Our faith and trust in God must grow stronger every day. Yes, there will be days we fall short, or maybe even weeks or months, but God is love. He is forgiving, and He wants us to return to Him and follow his ways. I thank God that He loves all of us unconditionally and wants an intimate relationship with every one of us, regardless of who we are, where we have been, and what we have done. Seeking God needs to be our Number One priority!

## THE "700 CLUB"

I have suffered with digestion issues for years. I heard about a food and nutrition book on our local PBS station. It sounded interesting, so I bought a copy. As I began to read, I had the strangest sense that my buying this book was divinely inspired. I felt as if God was speaking to me through this book.

The main issue for me seemed to be gluten. I had considered this before and half-heartedly tried to cut some out of my diet, but realized that it had to be an all or nothing endeavor if I was to know what the true source of the problem was. John's dietician sister later confirmed my suspicions during a conversation about my symptoms. She told me that many of my symptoms were indicative of celiac disease, which is directly related to gluten intolerance.

This meant a complete diet overhaul. I went through every food product in my kitchen, noting what I could and couldn't eat. Gluten can be hidden, so it took me a couple of days and a lot of label reading to sort everything out.

On July 1, I officially began my gluten-free diet. It was hard for the first few days, because I had to give up some of my favorite foods, but I was determined to stick with it. My ninth day into a gluten-free life, God showed me I was on the right path.

It was late, and I was getting ready for bed. I turned on the TV in our bedroom. I was surprised to see the "700 Club" on my screen because I don't normally watch it. For some reason, I was transfixed. They were praying for people, and I felt as if I couldn't move. I watched, almost waiting for something to be said directly to me. Then I heard it. The woman began praying and said, "Someone is having digestion issues. They have had to change the way they are eating. The Lord wants you to know that He is healing you. He is bringing balance to the acids in your stomach." I can't even begin to explain how I felt at that moment. God had spoken to me, loud and clear, through this woman, giving me His promise of healing.

*O Lord my God, I called to you for help*
*and you healed me.*
Psalm 30:2

131

I stood there praising God as tears filled my eyes and ran down my cheeks. I felt so loved by God knowing that in the entire universe, He took the time to convey His love, compassion, and healing message for me. Once again, I was humbled and in awe of our Lord. Every time that God speaks to me in some way, shape or form, I am amazed at how close of a relationship He wants with us. I am no different from anyone else, other than I want intimacy with God. I want to know His desires for my life and me. So, I follow Him. I read His Word. I pray, and I try to be obedient when He tells me which path to take. I am not perfect in my walk with the Lord, and that's OK, He knows me, but He also knows my heart, and my heart yearns to know Him at the most intimate level.

In Chronicles 14, we read about how David's heart was bent toward God. Even though David made many mistakes, committing adultery and murder, **God honored what was in his heart, not his perfection.** We will never be perfect while on this earth, but God just wants our heart. He wants to know we value Him above all else. God will position us where He can use us best because He knows our hearts, not because we are "perfect" followers of Him.

God can and will speak to you when your heart and mind yearn to know Him and follow Him. He desires this for us, and nothing in this world can be better than to be connected to our Heavenly Father in a loving, intimate relationship. Reach out to Him and reap the rewards!

## POINTS TO PONDER

It's all about our hearts, and we never know what God is up to. Sometimes he wants to break our hearts, change our hearts, or soothe our hearts. Every situation we are in can teach us something different about God's heart.

- Has he broken your heart for the poor and needy? What steps have you taken to help in this area?

- Has he shown you that you need a "change of heart?" Are you still prideful? Stubborn? Unforgiving? How can you start changing one of these issues?

- Has he spoken directly to you and given you a grateful heart? Name five things you are grateful to God for.

- Do you know what is "near and dear" to God's heart? How much time have you spent reading God's Word? Do you see the relevance in knowing God's heart through His Word?

Next time you are in prayer, ask God to speak to your heart and fill it with His desires, His longings, and His compassion.

*So I say to you: Ask and it will be given to you;*
*seek and you will find; knock and the door will be*
*opened to you. For everyone who asks receives; and*
*he who seeks finds; and to him who knocks, the*
*door will be opened.*

Luke 11:9-10

CHAPTER ELEVEN

# God is Personal

God is a very personal God—above all else, He wants a relationship with us. He wants a direct phone line to us and wants us to call Him regularly. Just as when we call up our friends and family, God expects us to take the time to speak with Him telling Him all our worries and problems. He also wants us to praise and worship Him for all the blessings that He gives to us.

There really isn't any difference other than we can't "physically" see the Lord; we believe that He is up there in Heaven and that He watches over us, so why on earth do we think that we can't talk to Him just like we would a friend? Also, why would we think that the Almighty Father of Heaven and Earth wouldn't be able to respond to us in a way that we can hear Him?

To some people that may sound crazy, but for those of us who have already seen and heard God speak to us through others, the Bible, TV, radio, or numerous other methods of communication, we know it to be the truth. Anyone can hear from the Lord; He doesn't play favorites, but He does require us to have a personal relationship with Him.

Think about it this way. If you had a friend that you enjoyed spending time with and talking to who suddenly quit calling you, never came around, and who you were never able to get in touch with, wouldn't that friendship suffer? The communication would be broken, and you would not know what was going on in their life. I'm sure you would feel hurt and sad about it. That is how our Lord feels when we don't take time out of our day to talk with Him and share our innermost feelings. He knows everything about us, loves us unconditionally, and wants what is best for us, but it's hard for Him to share those things if we don't care to spend the time with Him. We work on other relationships in our lives with our spouses, our children, our family, our friends, and our co-workers, but we miss the most important one of all—the relationship with our Lord Jesus Christ!

If you want to be close to God, carve out some time in your day to spend with Him. I find the morning to be the best time because it starts my day with a wonderful, peaceful feeling of hope, love, and joy. You decide what time of day is best. God doesn't care because He is always there ready to listen. Spend some time in your Bible, and then spend some time in prayer. Start with 10 to 15 minutes a day until you develop a habit of doing it; then increase your time with God. Maybe cut out something else in your day that you really don't need to do, and give that extra time to God. You just need to start; you will be amazed at how God will respond to your obedience.

In the past twelve years having walked with the Lord, I have been blessed to see and hear the Lord speak to me in numerous ways and give me guidance for various things that I prayed about. Every time it happens, I am just as amazed as the first time I felt his presence with me. I want to share some of the small daily things that God has shown me revealing just how real he is, and how personal his guidance and answers are.

---

I wanted to go to a leadership conference but wasn't sure that I should spend the money on it because we were trying to get out of debt. The cost was $250. That same day, I received a letter from my doctor. Thinking that it was results from a regular screening, I opened it up to find a check for $140 for an overpayment. That never happened before. Then a friend called to order some vitamins I had in stock. When I totaled the amount, it came to $110. Together, these two checks equaled the exact amount that I needed for the conference. Praise God—he provided!

---

*I had just started taking a new probiotic and that night I had some terrible pains in my stomach. I asked the Lord to show me what it was causing my discomfort. The next morning I was watching the news, and a segment about adopting animals came on. I heard them say that the dog up for adoption was named "Chicory," which I thought was an odd name for a dog. Then I picked up my bottle of probiotics and looked at the list of ingredients. There was chicory root in the capsules. I realized that must be what upset my stomach the night before. God speaks in mysterious ways.*

---

I had been praying about whether or not I was supposed to go to a new doctor for about two months. I prayed, "Lord, please put it right in front of me." The next morning, a friend of mine came to visit. Handing me a business card she said, "Sharon this is for you, this is about you. My sister was feeling bad and went to a new doctor that she just loves, and she is already starting to feel better. The name on the card was the name of the doctor I had been praying about.

---

*I have been on my knees praying for someone and that person will either call or text me within minutes or hours. I asked God to let me know who needs some encouragement or ministering. Sure enough, I received a phone call from a friend who needed a listening ear about some problem in her life.*

I am not divinely graced with a secret direct line to God. Anyone can experience this, as illustrated below.

## THE JOB OPPORTUNITY OF A LIFETIME?

This story is from a friend of ours who for years has skirted the issue of hearing from God. I have told him my "God stories." He has always thought they were amazing, but never imagined that he would one day experience a God story himself. Here is his story.

HOGWASH, POPPYCOCK, VOODOO—I have to admit, I wasn't a believer. I wasn't one of those people who thought God had the time or telepathic powers to send me individual signs; to communicate with us in some sort of otherworldly manner. Jesus talking to me? Yea, right. But the summer of 2008 changed all that. The company that I had worked at for 25 years was bought out by a global giant. I watched thousands of my co-workers get fired, laid-off, or leave. A few years later, I decided to accept a buyout and pursue other options.

One of those was with a thriving company in Colorado that I had worked with over the years. They were promising me everything I wanted and a chance to head up my own department. Everything seemed perfect, the stars had aligned, and I was feeling very fortunate. The president of the company wined and dined my wife and me, being the perfect gentleman during our discussions. He promised that it would be an awesome adventure, and we would take the company to new heights. He was winning me over.

However, he did have a reputation for being tough to work for and hard to please. So, I boldly confronted him about it. He assured me that he was a changed man, and we would make a great team. Imagine my dilemma; should I accept this new position in a new city and take my chances, or should I listen to several employees who warned me to beware? I was riddled with doubt and didn't know who to trust. The clock was ticking, and I had to give an answer within weeks. So, I turned to some friends who offered this advice: pray about it and ask God to give you a sign to help you make the right decision. They assured me that God would hear my prayers and answer me. Me, turning to God? Praying for a "sign?" It sounded crazy, but out of desperation, I followed their advice. I started praying constantly; I read the Bible for the first time in years, and I signed up for an online devotional. I gave my life to God and asked for help and amazing things began to happen.

During a random trip out of town, I miraculously ran into one of the president's assistants. She spoke to me confidentially and uttered the words I will never forget, "A leopard doesn't change its spots!" She told me, among other things, that he was putting his best foot forward because he really wanted me to work for him. Since we barely knew each other, I had to wonder why she would confide in me with all this information about her boss. So I tucked this new information away and kept praying, asking God for more signs. Should I stay or should I go? Suddenly, signs began appearing everywhere; I would get in my car, turn on the radio, and hear the announcer talking about Colorado; I would walk into the health club for a quick workout, and a woman right in front of me had on a t-shirt with one word—Colorado! I was convinced that God was answering my prayers—but not so fast! The same friends who told me to start praying and asking God for signs assured me that

I needed to slow down. I needed to get into the Bible and make sure the signs were directly tied into scriptures in the Bible. Then I would know for sure where God was leading me.

A lot of time had passed, and I was more confused than ever. I was down to only 48 hours before I had to give my decision; one that could change my life forever. I randomly decided to call the woman whom I had spoken with weeks earlier hoping to ask her more questions about the job, the company, and the president. After a 15-minute conversation with her, I thanked her for her honesty and her time, and then it happened again. Just as I was getting ready to hang up, she uttered those memorable words again: "Remember, Jim, a leopard doesn't change its spots!" That same night, a friend encouraged me to sign up for Rick Warren's daily devotional. Why not? I need all the spirituality I can get, so I signed up expecting to get my first devotional a few days later. It was Friday night, and I had until Sunday to give my answer. I was considering saying yes but my stomach was in knots.

Saturday morning, I was wide awake by 5:30 a.m. I was stressed, so I grabbed my laptop to read my emails. To my surprise, my first daily devotional from Rick Warren had arrived. Wow that was fast!

I checked my other emails first, however, deciding to leave his for later. Just as I was closing my laptop, I heard a small voice say, "Open Rick Warren's devotional NOW!" Ok, what the heck! I opened it and began reading. I almost fell over! I was stunned and dumbfounded. These were the words staring back at me. They hit me like a ton of bricks:

*Can an ethiopian change his skin or a leopard its spots? Neither can you do good who are accustomed to doing evil.* Jeremiah 13:23

This can't be, I thought. Impossible. Within seconds I realized those were the exact words the president's assistant had told me on several different occasions. More importantly, I had no idea that "saying" was actually a scripture in the Bible. Then I remembered what my friend had told me; look for important signs embedded in the scriptures to make sure it was from God. Well, that was it—My Sign! I woke up my wife and told her that we were NOT going to Colorado!

Twenty-four hours later, I called the president in Colorado and told him I wasn't taking the job. I would stay in St. Louis and strike out on my own. I asked God for a sign, and he put up a billboard for me saying, "Hello, Jim! This is God speaking; do not trust the guy in Colorado. Stay in St. Louis!" Today, some four years later, it was the best decision I could have made, for many reasons, all of which God already knew.

Unbeknownst to everyone, my father had a brain tumor. The same week I would have started in Colorado, my father collapsed. He was given little time to live and, sadly, passed away just three months later. My mother is now gone, too, but because I stayed in St. Louis, I was able to spend a lot of time with her before she died. The business I started has also flourished from zero clients to steady, continuous work within a variety of industries. More importantly than that, I realized that once I asked God to come into my life and show me the way, he led me down a path that tested my faith, my belief, and my commitment. God brought people, places, and circumstances into my life that were too unique to simply be called coincidences! Here's the best part of my journey. A leopard may not change its spots, but I have changed. I'm now a believer—a believer in the power of prayer, the meaning of signs, and in our Lord Jesus Christ. It has been amazing, and I continue to speak all the time with God!

## THE HOUSE OFF THE HIGHWAY

A dear friend of mine encountered God in an interesting way—here is her story of God intervening in the life of a stranger.

One day as I drove home from work, I noticed a house off to the side of the highway. There was nothing unusual about it, but my eyes were drawn toward it. The next day, the same thing happened only this time something non-descript captured my attention. As I approached the house on the third day, God spoke to me and told me to pray for the people that live there. On the fourth day, God spoke to me telling me to go to the house! I thought, "That is totally crazy. I am not going to that house. I could get killed." I quickly dismissed the voice of God, knowing I must have misunderstood Him. However, as I got into my car the next morning, I heard God speak again. I stopped what I was doing and said aloud, "God, if this is really you, out of obedience I will go to that house this afternoon."

Well, God wasted no time that afternoon in convincing me I needed to go to that house. I was panic stricken! As I got closer to my destination, I felt the temperature climbing in my car. God's presence was heavy. I sat in my car in front of this house praying for protection and asking for strength and courage. I slowly walked up to the door, gasping for breath, asking the Holy Spirit to prompt my speech. I rang the doorbell. I heard a man's voice respond. He did not open the door, so I said, "Sir, I drive past your house every day; and the Lord told me to pray for whoever lives here. Now He is compelling me to speak with you directly." After a long pause, he finally responded with, "Are you an angel?" I laughed and assured him I was not. He then opened the door and invited me in. I felt that someone else was also in the house, and at that moment, a woman started down the long staircase. God began speaking to her through me.

She was a minister's wife. Because of an incredibly challenging time she and her husband were going through at church, she had secluded herself in her home. She couldn't bear the thought of leaving and had become ill due to stress. As God reinforced the details of their lives, I realized I was there to "minister" to them because I had just emerged from the same season of challenge. I, too, was a minister's wife and had "secluded" myself during a difficult time. I was able to encourage them and pray for them in their distress. God used my experience to comfort another woman, who was a stranger to me. It was a miraculous time of healing. As I drove home that night, I was mesmerized by what God had done. He used me in my obedience to Him and touched someone's life.

I continued to stay in touch with her through email, and marveled at how God would repeatedly have me pray for her on issues that she struggled with in her life. His timing was perfect, as always, and she was able to begin healing. She was extremely thankful to the Lord for providing a "stranger" to console her in her time of need. On our journey with God, we can expect to hear His promptings and voice speaking to us. We just need to listen!

---

My question to you is, "Are You Listening?"

- Do you believe that God is real and that He can and does speak to you in your everyday life?
- Are you willing to open your heart to Him and have a relationship with Him?
- Are you willing to open your eyes and ears to hear what He has to say to you?
- Are you willing to have the faith and trust that it takes to believe in all these possibilities?
- Are you willing to take some time out of your hectic schedule and go spend time with the Lord?

I pray that you are willing and that you will hold tight to the truth that the one who created the universe cares about every aspect of your life. He wants you to listen for his direction and encouragement. He promises to walk with you, and send His Spirit to help you listen and discern his will. I pray that you will find joy in devoting time to grow your relationship and your faith in Jesus Christ. I pray that you look forward to reading God's Word daily and commit to responding in obedience to what the Holy Spirit reveals to you. Pray this prayer:

*Heavenly Father, I come to you humbly and boldly in the name of Jesus Christ, your Son, my Savior. I thank and praise you for your undeserved love that you pour out on me daily. I thank you for your forgiveness for all the times I have not listened for your voice or to your message. Open the eyes and ears of my faith to seek your will and to truly listen for your voice and direction. As you have given your all —your life—for me, Jesus, I give my life to you. Teach me. Direct me. Speak to me. I am listening. In the name of Jesus I pray. Amen.*

In closing, my hope is that you will be encouraged to seek God, read His Word, the Bible, and spend some quiet time with Him in prayer. Then, you will find out for yourself how miraculous a relationship with Him can be, and how He will reveal to you his peace and love and divine grace. Praise God!

## POINTS TO PONDER

Do you really believe that God will speak to you? You must have the faith to believe this, otherwise you will not see it when it happens. A heart that trusts in the Lord will have open eyes and ears for seeing and hearing. So, you have some choices to make.

- Will you start seeking God daily? Ask God to help you want to know Him more intimately.

- How much time will you devote to your relationship with God each day? How important do you think this is?

- Will you read the Bible and pray each day? What are your priorities in life? Do they include God?

- Will you obediently listen and respond to what God shows you? Are you a person who will follow through on an issue, and what could this mean in your walk with God?

It's all up to you. God will not force you to do anything. I pray that you are encouraged today to begin to take your relationship with our Heavenly Father seriously, and make Him a priority in your life.

GOD BLESS YOU!

# PERSONAL BIBLE STUDY SCRIPTURES

Reading God's Word is one way to get to know him better. I pray that you will study these scriptures and let God speak to your heart.

## CHAPTER ONE

Job 33:14

"For God speaks again and again, though people do not recognize it."

2 Timothy 1:7

"For God did not give us a spirit of fear, but a spirit of power, love, and of self-discipline."

Ephesians 3:20

"Now to him (God) who is able to do immeasurably more than all we ask or imagine, according to his power that is at work within us."

Matthew 11:15

"He who has ears, let him hear"

Jeremiah 29:11-13

"For I know the plans I have for you," declares the Lord, "Plans to prosper you and not to harm you, plans to give you hope and a future. Then you will call upon me and come and pray to me, and I will listen to you. You will seek me and find me when you seek me with all your heart."

## CHAPTER TWO

Deuteronomy 31:8

"The Lord himself goes before you and will be with you; he will never leave you nor forsake you. Do not be afraid; do not be discouraged."

Isaiah 40:31

"But those who hope in the Lord will renew their strength. They will soar on wings like eagles; they will run and not grow weary, they will walk and not be faint."

Romans 5: 3-4

"Not only so, but we also rejoice in our sufferings, because we know that suffering produces perseverance; perseverance, character; and character, hope."

## CHAPTER THREE

Psalm 121: 1-2

"I lift up my eyes to the hills—where does my help come from? My help comes from the Lord, the Maker of heaven and earth."

Isaiah 46:4

"Even to your old age and gray hairs I am he, I am he who will sustain you. I have made you and I will carry you; I will sustain you and I will rescue you."

Hebrews 4:13

"Nothing in all creation is hidden from God's sight. Everything is uncovered and laid bare before the eyes of him to whom we must give account."

## CHAPTER FOUR

Matthew 6:33

"But seek first his kingdom and his righteousness, and all these things will be given to you as well."

Psalm 86:10

"For you are great and do marvelous deeds;
you alone are God."

Hebrews 1:2

"...in these last days he has spoken to us by his Son,
whom he appointed heir of all things, and through
whom he made the universe."

## CHAPTER FIVE

Genesis 1:1

"In the beginning, God created the heavens and the earth."

Genesis 1:31

"God saw all that he had made, and it was very good."

Proverbs 4:11-12

"I guide you in the way of wisdom and lead you along straight paths. When you walk, your steps will not be hampered; when you run, you will not stumble."

John 1:16

"From the fullness of his grace we have all received
one blessing after another."

## CHAPTER SIX

Philippians 4:6-7

"Do not be anxious about anything, but in everything, by prayer and petition, with thanksgiving, present your requests to God. And the peace of God, which transcends all understanding, will guard your hearts and minds in Christ Jesus."

Hebrews 11:1

"Now faith is being sure of what we hope for and certain of what we do not see."

Romans 8:28

"And we know that in all things God works for the good of those who love him, who have been called according to his purpose."

## CHAPTER SEVEN

Daniel 6:23

"The king was overjoyed and gave orders to lift Daniel out of the den. And when Daniel was lifted from the den, no wound was found on him, because he had trusted in his God."

Psalm 82:3

"Defend the cause of the weak and fatherless; maintain the rights of the poor and oppressed."

## CHAPTER EIGHT

Mark 11:24

"Therefore I tell you, whatever you ask for in prayer, believe that you have received it, and it will be yours."

1 John 3:17

"If anyone has material possessions and sees his brother in need but has no pity on him, how can the love of God be in him?"

Romans 9:1-2

"I speak the truth in Christ—I am not lying, my conscience confirms it in the Holy Spirit—I have great sorrow and unceasing anguish in my heart."

## CHAPTER NINE

Jeremiah 33:3

"Call to me and I will answer you and tell you great and un-searchable things you do not know."

Acts 2:44-45

"Now all who believed were together, and had all things in common, and sold their possessions and goods, and divided them among all, as anyone had need."

## CHAPTER TEN

ISAIAH 58:11

"The Lord will guide you always; he will satisfy your needs in a sun-scorched land and will strengthen your frame. You will be a well-watered garden, like a spring whose waters never fail."

PSALM 30:2

"O Lord my God, I called to you for help and you healed me."

## CHAPTER ELEVEN

LUKE 11:9-10

"So I say to you: Ask and it will be given to you; seek and you will find; knock and the door will be opened to you. For everyone who asks receives; and he who seeks finds; and to him who knocks, the door will be opened."

# ABOUT THE AUTHOR

Sharon Anderson spent 25 years in the fitness industry as a fitness trainer and nutritionist. While she thoroughly enjoyed helping people feel better and become healthier, God clearly showed her a new career path—that of author. She left fitness and dedicated herself to writing her first book, *God Speaks: Are You Listening?* She hopes God will continue to work through her to encourage others to seek God and the purpose for their lives.

Sharon is married to John, a wonderful, God-fearing man, who is her best friend and biggest supporter. She is a mother of two children, a son and daughter, who currently live near her in St. Louis, Missouri. She is blessed to be a "Nana" to five beautiful granddaughters and spends as much time with them as possible. She loves to nurture the relationship with each one and hopes to leave a legacy with them of putting God first in their lives.

Sharon has experienced God's loving hand in her life for the past 14 years and the experiences have been life-changing. She loves sharing "God stories" and plans on writing more books to help others understand how real He is in their lives and how He speaks with them daily.

Some of her hobbies are walking, biking, hiking and yoga. She loves the outdoors and cooking. She also has a passion for interior decorating and has renovated their last three homes.

She is always ready to travel with her husband, especially to places where they can volunteer and fulfill a need in caring for others as witnesses for God. They have taken several mission trips to Mexico and Africa and feel it is such a blessing to minister to others for God. They also enjoy recreational travel to small, quaint towns and mountainous surroundings. They both feel a sense of God in all of creation, but most especially in nature.

## CONNECT WITH SHARON

Would you like to keep in contact with Sharon and read her blogs? You can also send in your own personal "God" stories. She would love to hear from you.

Visit her at:
Sharonmarieanderson.com

Or email her at:
Sharon@sharonmarieanderson.com